Very interesting -

FRONTIER FIGHTERS

MAJOR WALTER JAMES CUMMING

Frontier Fighters

On Active Service in Waziristan

EDITED BY

JULES STEWART

Pen & Sword
MILITARY

First published in Great Britain in 2010 by
Pen & Sword Military
an imprint of
Pen & Sword Books Ltd
47 Church Street
Barnsley
South Yorkshire
S70 2AS

Editorial matter copyright © Jules Stewart 2010

ISBN: 978-1-84884-241-0

The right of Ruby Mukhia to be identified as Literary Executor and of
Jules Stewart as Editor of this Work has been asserted by them in
accordance with the Copyright, Designs and Patents Act 1988.

A CIP catalogue record for this book is
available from the British Library.

Typeset in 11/13pt Sabon by
Concept, Huddersfield, West Yorkshire

Printed and bound in England by
the MPG Books Group

Pen & Sword Books Ltd incorporates the Imprints of Pen & Sword
Aviation, Pen & Sword Maritime, Pen & Sword Military, Wharncliffe
Local History, Pen & Sword Select, Pen & Sword Military Classics,
Leo Cooper, Remember When, Seaforth Publishing and Frontline
Publishing.

For a complete list of Pen & Sword titles please contact
PEN & SWORD BOOKS LIMITED
47 Church Street, Barnsley, South Yorkshire, S70 2AS, England
E-mail: enquiries@pen-and-sword.co.uk
Website: www.pen-and-sword.co.uk

Contents

Foreword

Major Cumming's memoirs took me back to my soldiering days on the North-West Frontier. During my Army days in Pakistan, I served in the Chitral Scouts, Tochi Scouts, Zhob Militia and also as ADC to the Governor of the North-West Frontier Province. This provided me with a comprehensive view of life on the Frontier and I got to know in depth the various Pathan tribes who inhabit this mostly inhospitable territory. Reading through this young British officer's experiences brought to mind rather strikingly how little things had changed several decades later, when I had to deal with the rebellious yet fascinating Pathan tribesmen. I say 'fascinating' because in spite of their warlike and intractable nature, and the trouble they caused us, British officers respected the tribesmen's toughness and proud character, as well as their bravery in battle.

It seems quite uncanny how little things have changed in Pakistan's tribal territory. If the tribesmen were a handful for the British in Cumming's days, as well as for the Pakistan government after Partition when I served on the Frontier, Pakistan's tribal belt today represents an even greater threat to stability, and not just on a local level. In the days of the British Raj, soldiers like Cumming had to contend with parties of tribesmen staging raids in the Settled Districts or on military outposts. The punitive expeditions and pitched battles that would follow are described in dramatic detail in Cumming's memoirs. Years later, we also had to deal with ambushes when we were out on *gasht*, or patrol, and Pathan raiders were still crossing the administrative border to steal whatever weapons or goods they could lay their hands on.

Today the tribal belt known as Federally Administered Tribal Areas (FATA) poses a threat on a much greater scale. For one thing, the tribesmen possess a highly sophisticated and lethal arsenal, and they have demonstrated their ability to use these weapons with deadly skill. More critical is the fact that FATA has become a sanctuary for Taliban insurgents and Al Qaeda militants, the home-grown variety as well as those who infiltrate across the porous border with Afghanistan. FATA has now become a menace on a global scale and President Barack Obama was right to call it 'the most dangerous place on Earth'.

Major Cumming's memoirs provide a valuable insight into the tribesmen's character, in particular that of the Mahsuds who are without a doubt the most fanatical and unyielding of the Pathan tribes. It is widely believed that Osama bin Laden and his henchmen are holed up in Waziristan, which is the Mahsuds' homeland. These are the reminiscences of a British soldier who spent most of his career at close quarters with the people who now offer shelter to the world's most dangerous terrorists. The memoirs make enlightening reading for military and political leaders, historians, academics or anyone in the general public who wishes to gain a deeper understanding of this conflict zone.

Colonel Tony Streather OBE

Acknowledgements

My thanks go first and foremost to Margaret Brown, who most generously granted permission to reproduce the photos for this book from the albums of her late husband, Major Willy Brown of the South Waziristan Scouts. Of course, there would have been no book without the memoirs. Wholehearted thanks must go to Major Cumming's adopted son, Ruby Mukhia, who made the typescript available to me on a trip to Darjeeling. My gratitude to my editor, Bobby Gainher, for diligently spotting the usual howlers and for his overall improvement of the text, and to Pen & Sword for taking on the manuscript. Whatever light my editorial comments may shed on the business of soldiering in Waziristan largely reflects the knowledge I gained in conversation with former Frontiersmen, Colonel Tony Streather, Graham Wontner-Smith, Major John Girling and Rodney Bennett. Lastly, thanks go as usual to my agent Duncan McAra. Had it not been for his efforts I would almost certainly remain an unpublished author.

Introductory Reminiscences
by Colonel (Retd) Kushqat ul Mulk

The four incidents recorded below by Colonel Kushqat ul Mulk, now ninety-six, a former Commandant of the South Waziristan Scouts, the unit in which Major Cumming served, convey the humour and humanity that often characterized a soldier's life on the receiving end of the Pathan *jezail*, or long-barrel musket. His anecdotes bring to mind a remark by the late George MacDonald Fraser, the creator of Flashman, who once said that 'war can also be funny'.

I joined the South Waziristan Scouts (SWS) in 1941 from Singapore and subsequently served as a Wing Officer, Wing Commander and Second in Command until 1946 when I was posted to my army battalion. In 1946, I went back to the SWS as its Commandant. It may be instructive for the reader to learn of a few episodes I experienced while serving in the SWS.

While travelling to Ladha in a convoy of two armoured lorries, the leading truck in which I was sitting in the front seat, while going around a bend, tumbled into the river. It was just below Mairobi village, short of Makin. The village of Mairobi belonged to the Shabi Khel tribe whose head, the notorious Mullah Powindah, had in the past given us a rather tough time. While the troops in the second truck took up positions on the hills above the road, the JCO in my truck and I collected all those injured in the fall and we didn't really know what to do next. In the meanwhile the Shabi Khel tribesmen from Mairobi ran down to the fallen truck and took great pains to pull it out of the river and place it on the road facing towards Ladha. I mention this as an example of Divine Mercy and also to shed some light on people who may otherwise have opposing views, but who were willing to extend help in a tricky situation.

While in Ladha post we received orders to demolish a tower across the river where a notorious hostile tribesman had been hiding. It took us nearly a month to issue warning notices to the villagers, through the political authorities headed by tehsildar Gul Mohammad. On his assurance that the village was now ready for the shelling operation, the guns were ordered to direct their aim at the tower only. After several shells were fired at the tower I gave up the operation, thinking it to be a futile exercise because of the small size of the one tower, and went off to the officers' mess for a drink. I had barely finished my first drink when news came in that the tower had fallen and only then did I realize that our artillery shells had been on target. We always took great pains to pinpoint our target and avoid the kind of collateral damage that some find acceptable in current operations.

This happened in Tiarza during the time that the Faqir of Ipi was a menace to us. Although he operated mostly in north Waziristan and seldom appeared in Mahsud-dominated south Waziristan, he surfaced one day in Tiarza and we came under his shelling at our post. These were solid iron balls which would hit the object and break it with their weight and velocity. The shelling frightened Jeffrey, the fox terrier of Major French, the British Wing Commander of Tiarza. The dog scurried to hide behind the furniture. Although some of the garrison took positions on the walls of the fort most of them started looking for Jeffery, out of fear of inviting the wrath of Major French. It was only after they found Jeffery behind a sofa that they seriously started the operation against Ipi's attacking force.

When I was in Jandola I received news that the Mahsuds had collected in strength near Kotkai on the road to Sararogha, eight miles beyond Jandola. They had even started sniping at our Kotkai post. I rushed in with reinforcements to Kotkai. While returning fire at the Mahsuds my troops discovered a comb of honey inside the rocks. I soon noticed that the attention of quite a number of my troops had quite cheerfully been diverted from dodging sniper fire to collecting honey.

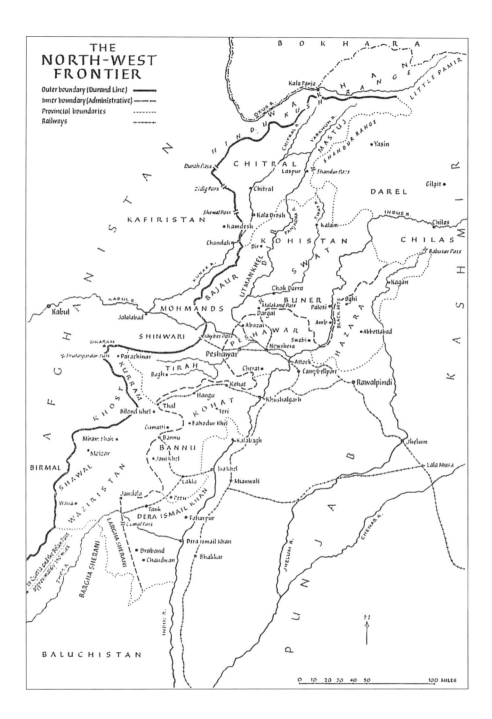

THE
NORTH-WEST
FRONTIER

Outer boundary (Durand Line) ⎯⎯⎯
Inner boundary (Administrative) ⎯ ⎯ ⎯
Provincial boundaries ⋯⋯⋯⋯
Railways ⊢⊢⊢⊢

B O K H A R A

H I N D U   K U S H   R A N G E

LITTLE PAMIR

Kala Panja

OXUS R.

CHITRAL R.

YARKHUN R.

MASTUJ

SHANDUR RANGE

Yasin

CHITRAL

Durah Pass

Laspur

Shandur Pass

Gilgit

Zidig Pass

Chitral

DAREL

INDUS R.

Shewal Pass

Kala Drosh

SWAT R.

PANJKORA R.

kalam

Chilas

KAFIRISTAN

Kamdesh

K O H I S T A N

CHILAS

Chandak

Dir

Babusar Pass

KUMAR R.

BAJAUR

UTMANKHEL

S W A T

Kagan

Chak Darra

Oghi

BLACK MTS.

KABUL R.

MOHMANDS

BUNER

Palosi

H A Z A R A

Kabul

Jalalabad

Kataland Pass

Dargai

Amb

Abbettabad

SHINWARI

Abazai

P E S H A W A R

Swabi

A F G H A N I S T A N

SIKARAM

Khyber Pass

Newshra

Shutargardar Pass

Parachinar

Peshawar

TIRAH

Chtrat

Attock

Campbellpur

Rawalpindi

Bagh

Kohat

KURAM

KHOST

Hangu

Khushalgarh

Biland khel

Thal

K O H A T

Teri

Jhelum

Camatti

Bahodur Khel

Miram Shah

Bannu

Kalabagh

K A S H M I R

Maizar

B A N N U

Jani Khel

Lala Musa

BIRMAL

SHAWAL

Isakhel

Mianwali

W A Z I R I S T A N

Lakla

Jandola

Pezu

Wana

Tank

DERA ISMAIL KHAN

Fotharpur

LARGHA SHERANI

Gamal Pass

Draband

Dera Ismail Khan

BARGHA SHERANI

Chaudwan

Bhakkar

INDUS R.

JHELUM R.

CHENAB R.

P U N J A B

to Quetta and the mountain territory under military tribes

ZHOB R.

BALUCHISTAN

N

0 10 20 30 40 50   100 MILES

xi

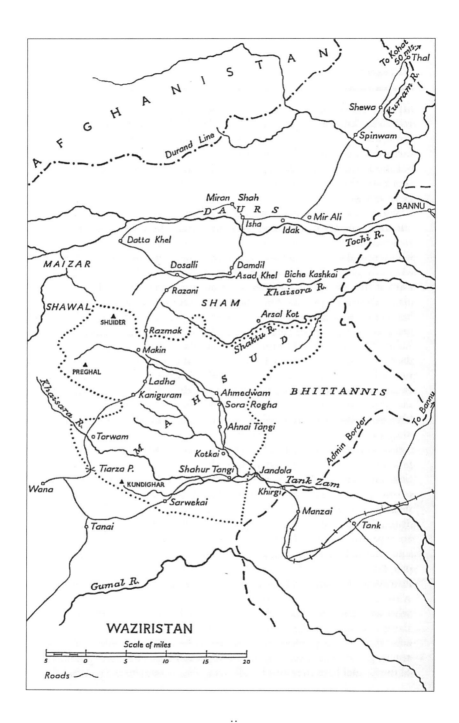

WAZIRISTAN

Scale of miles

5   0   5   10   15   20

Roads

Introduction

When in 1915 Walter James Cumming, age eighteen, journeyed on the dusty, mountainous road to Quetta to be interviewed for a commission in the Indian Army, the North-West Frontier of British India was enjoying a rare period of calm. In the previous three-quarters of a century since the British had taken control of the Punjab, and with it the wild Frontier territory, the Army had fought more than fifty full-scale campaigns against the Pathan tribesmen, as well as a second major war with Afghanistan. Not a single armed conflict had taken place since 1908, although the year of Cumming's commissioning did see a brief outbreak of trouble with the Mohmand tribe that inhabits the hills north of the Khyber Pass. But that was hundreds of miles from Quetta, today the capital of Pakistan's Baluchistan Province.

Cumming was to see more than his share of action as a young officer alongside the South Waziristan Scouts, one of the native militias raised to keep the peace in the rugged tribal land adjoining India's turbulent Afghan border. As the young British officer was to learn, life on the Frontier was not all about hunting partridge and partying in the officers' mess, although there was plenty of that. It was a tough and dangerous life. An Indian Army officer was given two months' privilege pay on full leave for each year of service. For those serving on the Frontier this was extended to three months, in recognition of what was considered an extreme hardship posting. Despite the dangers, Frontier life held an undeniable allure for a young soldier seeking adventure, as well as a rapid rise through the ranks.

1

The Scouts were made up of Pathan tribesmen who, for the privilege of carrying a modern rifle and drawing a modest pay, were persuaded to fight for the British Raj against their own people. These levies came into being from the late 1870s onward, as an offshoot of the Corps of Guides that was raised by Lieutenant Sir Harry Lumsden in 1846 to protect the Frontier regions. Of all these militia units, the South Waziristan Scouts found themselves in the most precarious position. Other corps, such as the Khyber Rifles and the Mohmand Militia, were garrisoned close to Regular Army units that were able to provide support, if needed, whenever the native levies came under attack. Cumming and his troops were left out on a limb in a remote region of the Frontier, and they were facing the Mahsuds, the most recalcitrant and fearsome of the Pathan tribes whose character was, in the opinion of one Frontier administrator, 'arrogant, pig-headed and faithless'. This disdain was shared by many British officers who served on the Frontier, including Winston Churchill who dismissed the Pathans as a 'pestilential race'.

The novelist John Masters did a tour of duty with the 4th Gurkhas, during which time he took part in several Frontier skirmishes and set battles with this tribe. 'They never took prisoners but mutilated and beheaded any wounded or dead who fell into their hands,' he recalls in *Bugles and a Tiger*, his memoirs of the Frontier. 'They took advantage of the rules to disguise themselves as peaceful passers-by, or as women. They simulated death and pounced on anyone foolish enough to relax his guard.' A British Army officer lay severely wounded after a sharp battle and when he was found next day, 'he had been castrated and flayed, probably while alive, and his skin lay pegged out on the rocks not far from camp.' Masters recalls that if the Pathans captured any soldiers other than Muslims, and especially if the prisoners were Sikhs or British, they would routinely castrate and behead them. 'Both these operations were frequently done by the women. Sometimes they would torture prisoners with the death of a thousand cuts, pushing grass and thorns into each wound as it was made.' The tribesmen, and needless to say their women-folk, could pull even far more gruesome tortures out of their bag of tricks.

Yet there was another side to the coin. It seems almost inconceivable that these same Pathans could show unstinting loyalty to the very men whom their kinsmen would savagely mutilate on the battlefield. We come across this in one incident, when the Scouts were in full downhill retreat with the tribesmen firing straight into their backs as they ran. When Cumming's native orderly saw the bullets begin to kick up dust around him, he pulled off the young Englishman's topi and replaced it with his own turban to draw fire from the trophy their pursuers were trying to bag.

Cumming was serving with the Scouts when the Third Afghan War broke out in 1919, a conflict that incited the tribes to revolt along almost the entire length of the Frontier. In that year Cumming got a taste of full-scale Frontier warfare, of Pathan ambushes, the 'butcher and bolt' policy of retaliatory raids on villages in which homes were blown up and crops destroyed, unsparing hand-to-hand fighting, infernal heat, thirst and rampant outbreaks of disease and, finally, the aerial bombings by a fledgling RAF, a tactic that the tribesmen despised, but which brought the Afghan invaders to the negotiating table.

Cumming's memoirs shed light on a part of the world that, for the most part, has remained little changed since the early part of the past century when the young Englishman soldiered in these grim, hostile hills. The North-West Frontier Province of today 'belongs' to Pakistan, although as far as the tribal areas are concerned, the term must be taken with a pinch of salt. The Pathans, and in particular the Wazirs and Mahsuds of Waziristan, remain determined to hold on to their independence and tribal ways against all efforts to incorporate them into the mainstream of Pakistani society. Most of Cumming's career on the Frontier was spent engaging the Pathans in battle, and each day carried the threat of sudden, violent death. This experience left him with a deep respect for the tribesmen, as well as a love of Frontier life. There is no doubt that Cumming would have sympathized with a remark made by a British journalist who visited the Frontier in the 1950s. He called it 'the last free place on Earth'.

Walter James Cumming enlisted in the Indian Army nine months after the outbreak of the First World War in Europe. Having been born and brought up in Quetta, now part of Pakistan and in those days a remote outpost of the Indian Empire on the border with Afghanistan, Cumming joined the ranks of the Viceroy Commissioned Officers (VCOs) who served in Indian Army regiments, as opposed to King's Commissioned officers (KCOs), who were part of the British Army. By Cumming's day the Indian Army had been consolidated into a single fighting force. This came about in 1895 with the reorganization of the Bengal, Madras and Bombay presidency armies, which were in fact the inheritors of Britain's original colonial trading outposts, into four regional commands. Prior to the amalgamation, there were three commanders-in-chief and three lists of officers – an impressive duplication of functions, even by the standards of Indian bureaucracy. At the turn of the twentieth century, Lord Kitchener was Commander-in-Chief in India. Kitchener emerged victorious from a protracted and bitter power struggle with the Viceroy, Lord Curzon, and then proceeded to further streamline the armed forces of India, with the creation of Northern and Southern territorial commands. This gave the new Indian Army a fighting strength of 234,000 men, serving in nine divisions and eight cavalry brigades. By the start of the First World War, the Army had a combat strength of slightly more than 155,000 men; the ranks had swelled to nearly 600,000 troops, all volunteers, by the end of the war.

Cumming refers to relations with the Afghans across the border as being 'outwardly friendly' at the time of his enlistment. This was not always the case. Afghanistan never accepted the loss of Peshawar and the lands to the Indus River that lay across the Durand Line, as the official border that was demarcated in 1893 is known. Kabul exploited every opportunity to stir up trouble for the Raj, by inciting the border Pathan tribes to rebellion, after the British annexed the Punjab and North-West Frontier territories in 1849. The Government of India experienced some anxious moments at the outbreak of the First World War. A renewal of Afghan-inspired disturbances on the Frontier would have required the despatch of troops who were badly needed in other theatres of operations. There was also the fear that Turkey, which had entered the conflict on Germany's side, would coerce the Amir Habibullah into sending his mullahs to spread a wave of religious fanaticism amongst the tribes. The Amir did in fact entertain German as well as Turkish agents at Court, but he cunningly saw off pressures to support plans for an invasion of British India. Had Afghanistan declared war on Britain, there is little doubt that the Pathan tribes would have been incited to revolt, touching off a general conflagration on the Frontier.

Cumming later applied for a posting with one of the native militias which, starting in 1878 with the raising of the Khyber Rifles, had been formed on the Frontier. He was interviewed by an officer he refers to as Sir G.R. Keppel, who was Major General Sir George Roos-Keppel, Political Officer of the Khyber and later Chief Commissioner of the North-West Frontier. Roos-Keppel, a legend in his own time, epitomized the classic soldier-scholar, a man of Churchillian demeanour who, apart from keeping the peace on the Frontier, published a grammar of the Pashtu language, translated arcane Pathan historical manuscripts and co-founded Islamia College, today the undergraduate school of Peshawar University. Cumming was commissioned into the embryo force of what was to become the South Waziristan Scouts (SWS), a truly illustrious unit amongst North-West Frontier levies. The SWS was headquartered in one of the most dangerous parts of the Frontier, far from Regular Army units.

Chapter 1

The Making of a Frontiersman

In May 1915, after finishing with school-leaving examinations, my brother and I were taken along by Dad for an interview with the General Officer Commanding in Quetta,[1] where we both had been brought up. After asking us a few questions, the General told us that we would have to prove ourselves fit to serve in the Indian Army before he would recommend the granting of commissions. So for a couple of months we two youngsters were attached to a local Regiment, marched up and down the parade ground by a havildar of the unit,[2] taken on long route marches and thoroughly disciplined. The Commanding Officer of the unit must have given a satisfactory report on our training for we were both commissioned into the Indian Army Reserve on 1 August 1915.

My brother[3] left to join a unit stationed in a small outpost, Loralai, south of Fort Sandeman, and I departed to join an Indian Regiment in Chaman, a small military station on the border of British Baluchistan with Afghanistan.[4] The unit I found myself with did not take soldiering seriously and we junior officers were left much to ourselves, with lots of time to go shooting and for playing games. Chaman is at the southern end of the main trade route running from Kabul through Kandahar into Baluchistan, with the result that the small but crowded bazaar was a wonderful sight on any day that a camel caravan arrived. On those days, the small cantonment[5] fairly reeked of camels and the cries of traders, and their bargaining filled the air. Carpets, really beautiful carpets, could be had for a song, also *poshtins*,[6] warm Gilgit boots, large camel bags and gaudy-coloured waistcoats, embroidered with gold thread.

It was luck for the carefree, happy-go-lucky Regiment I was with that peace, perfect peace, reigned in Chaman in those days. Our only worry was thieving, the bazaar being a rendezvous for trans-border murderers, thieves and other bad hats, and in addition, no doubt, to a few from our side. There seemed to be very little check on the monthly population of the bazaar area. However, I must admit, this mixed crew of cut-throats troubled us military folk little, as they confined their attention to the rich shops of the local traders, whether Hindu or Mussalman, when loot was their objective. The border, running as it did within a few hundred yards of the cantonment, was no obstacle and could be crossed at any time by anyone. All Army personnel had strict orders not to wander across into Afghanistan. However, were one in pursuit of a wounded *kiloor*[7] or hare, the excitement of the chase could hardly deter the keen shikari[8] from trespassing over a border, marked rather haphazardly by distantly positioned pillars. Also, there was no border guard to say 'Nay', or at any rate I never saw one.

Our relations with the Afghans were, in those days, friendly, at least outwardly so, and therefore there was little reason for all the officers who were present with the Regiment to stay in Chaman at weekends. The more senior and older officers of the unit usually went for long weekends in search of wine, women and song to Quetta, only a few hours away by train, the timings of which appeared to have been fixed with these weekends in view.

Those of us young second lieutenants whose ambition was to serve in the Indian Army, after the termination of the war, were now given the choice of resigning our temporary commissions and attending a Cadet College for a few months, with a good prospect of gaining permanent commissions. I opted for this at once and so did my brother, and we met again at the Cadet College in Chaman in January 1916.

Life was now really strenuous, from early morning to evening with PT, parades, riding lessons, lectures and so on. I shall never forget the agony of early morning rifle exercise parades in January and February, with the temperature hovering well below the freezing mark, with snow on the ground and an icy wind whistling through the quad. With hands blue and benumbed, it was sheer torture. However we had a really grand lot of British NCO instructors, who were certainly not of the hard-fisted, bawling stamp one sometimes hears and reads about. One hundred and twenty of us were put through the course and I, for one, thoroughly enjoyed it. Only one incident occurred which marred our stay there and this was towards the end of our six months' training. The cadet platoon to which I was attached had the morning out for field sketching on horseback. All the Cadet College horses were dear old smokes, who understood and obeyed instantly all orders, from W-A-L-K to G-A-L-L-O-P, given by our riding master, but the horses given that morning for our exercise were, I think, borrowed from some unit in the station. At any rate, I found that the only way to do my sketch was to dismount now and again. My charger refused to stand still and several of my companions were faced with the same problem. After completing our road maps five of us turned back to return to College. We were trotting along together on the soft tan ride which ran alongside the tarmac road when, without warning, one of the horses, having decided that its time had come and gone, made up its mind to gallop back to the stables. Away he went, with his rider unable to hold him back. The rest of the horses in our group, not to be left behind, joined in the mad rush for home. No amount of pulling on the reins or sawing at the mouth had the slightest effect and the uncontrolled race continued for half a mile. So long as the soft tan ride lasted all was well but unfortunately for our horses and ourselves it stopped short, with a row of trees and a garden wall blocking the way ahead. At this point riders on the tan had to switch off sharply to the left and proceed on the main hard tarmac road. This was our undoing. My horse was number two in this hectic rush and about 10 yards behind the leader. Without slackening speed and yet switching off sharply resulted in the legs of the horses flying away from under them when their steel-shod hooves failed to grip on the slippery surface. Five horses and five cadets piled up in a struggling mass and by the time we had managed to get painfully on our feet the horses had recovered and continued on their gallop in a thunderous clatter.

A *garry*[9] happened to come along a minute or two later and the Pathan driver, seeing the bloodstained and woebegone group, had pity on us and transported us to the College hospital. We were all admitted, smeared with stinging iodine, smothered in bandages and put to bed all in the same ward. The following morning, still feeling very sorry for ourselves, the five of us were further shaken to the core when the austere form of the Colonel Commandant appeared at the door of the ward. Screwing his monocle more firmly into his eye he came forward a few steps to halt in front of our five beds. Then, after snorting 'Bloody young fools, not fit to ride donkeys!' he stamped out of the ward. As none of us had taken a 'voluntary' but had come down with his mount we considered his findings a bit unfair. The Riding Master of the College, a hard-bitten ranker major of a famous British cavalry regiment, never lost an opportunity to instil into us 'blockheads' that not one of us would ever be considered a rider until he had taken at least around a dozen good pearlers, and that sliding off the bare and very broad back of a riding school horse when riding facing its tail, and when the instructor without warning ordered T-R-O-T when walking, could not be considered one of the dozen. At any rate, the five of us who landed up in hospital after our mix-up felt that we had surely arrived on to the second rung of that twelve-rung ladder.

At the end of June 1916, the 120 of us, less perhaps half a dozen who failed to pass out on account of sickness or some other reason, piled into the Punjab Mail at Quetta station, each of us supporting a very new and glittering pip on each shoulder. This daily train was rudely referred to as the 'Heat Stroke Express' because not many months before a party of military personnel, travelling crowded in a third-class compartment in this Punjab Mail, had met with disaster: on arrival at a station on the line most of them were taken out suffering from heat stroke and not a few had died as a result.

Ever since that dreadful happening any compartment, whether first, second or third class, and carrying military personnel on the Punjab line, had to be provided with sufficient ice on the journey to keep the carriage temperature down. This applied only to the hot weather months, from April to September, and one of the railway guards on each train was responsible for seeing that the ice was replenished as necessary.

The following day, at Multan, those of us for units stationed on the North-West Frontier changed trains, while the rest of our friends, many of whom I never met again, went on to Lahore from where they would branch off in different directions. Providence decreed that my brother and I be posted to the same regiment, the 12th Frontier Force,[10] but to different battalions. He went to the 3rd Battalion and I was on my way to the 2nd. We parted company at Mari Indus station as he was bound for Kohat while I, with two others of the same group, was on my way to Bannu to join the same battalion.

We did not stay long in Mari as it was dreadfully hot and a most uninviting place. Collecting a few coolies for our kit, we walked over the sand to the bank of the Indus where we found a paddle steamer preparing to cross to Kalabagh. The Indus is always in flood during the months of May, June, July and August when the summer heat melts the snows of the Himalaya and the cold waters flow down to give welcoming respite to thousands living on her banks, and for some reason the west bank always seems a little cooler than the east.

The river being broader than usual and the current strong, the old ferry must have taken an hour to cross over, however the longer it took the happier we were. On the ferry was like being in an air-conditioned room, and in addition everything was strange to us and therefore interesting.

A short distance from the ferry stop we found the small Kalabagh refreshment room, which overlooked the swirling waters of the Indus and, for the first time since leaving Quetta, we enjoyed good meals in a cool atmosphere and congenial surroundings.

The head servant produced for our inspection and remarks a large book with well-thumbed pages, on the cover of which was printed 'Complaints Book'. However, within we found no complaints but numerous happy and witty remarks as well as a few short lyrics extolling the merits of the spic-and-span little rest house-cum-feeding house. It was going to be my lot to serve my King and Country many years across the Indus and further west across the administrative border of India[11] of the districts of Bannu, Dera Ghazi Khan, Dera Ismael Khan and Tank, and therefore many times later I stopped for meals and a refreshing rest in that delightful small riverside inn. Calling for the same 'Complaints Book', I would pore over the pages, enjoy the remarks and find many signatures of past and present friends of the Frontier.

A small narrow-gauge railway runs between Kalabagh and Bannu, with a branch line turning off to Tank (pronounced Tonk) from about halfway. Because of the fierce heat during the day we were taking the evening passenger train, but even so the compartment was like an oven and remained hot until about ten o'clock. There is no exaggeration in saying that the hot weather temperature in the barren and sun-baked lands of those districts of Bannu and Tank often soar up to an incredible 125° F. About twenty-five years later I served in the Western Desert and although the heat there during the daytime can be great, it can't hold a candle to that which Satan manages to stoke up in those godforsaken, semi-desolate lands bordering Waziristan.

At sundown it was time for the train to get on its way. The guard waved his green flag, at the same time blowing hard on his whistle. This was to warn passengers and their friends. The engine blew vast amounts of steam through its whistle, making a dreadful screech, but for half a minute nothing further happened. Apparently this was just another warning signal. However, soon after uttering another hideous screech the engine's pistons came to life and with many clanking jerks the train moved off. Full speed was around 15 to 20 mph.

I recollect that on one occasion when travelling on this line my Airedale pup, Paddy, catching sight of another dog close to the track as we puffed along at full speed, took a flying leap out of the window. I immediately pulled the communication cord, below which was a plate bearing the words 'Fine for Improper Use Rs50/–'. The little train obediently stopped, I raced back down the track and collected Paddy who, though shaken, was quite unhurt. The guard, with a kind and generous interpretation of the word 'improper', did not impose the fine. For this I was grateful. Subalterns seldom have 50 rupees to spare.

Our journey of considerably less than a hundred miles took us till a convenient hour the next morning when, at Bannu railway station, we were met by a tall jovial young officer, who informed us that he was the Adjutant. A fatigue party of men from the Battalion took charge of our kit and the four of us drove off in a tonga to the Bannu fort where we had our quarters. After a few minutes our kit arrived on a battalion mule cart and we were able to unpack, indulge in cold showers to wash away the sands of the journey and, getting into clean kit, we were ready to proceed to the Mess and meet our future fellow officers.

It was breakfast time and most of the battalion officers, including the Commanding Officer and Second in Command were present when we arrived at the Mess, so it did not take long to get the introductions over. Received with great friendliness, we were soon made to feel at home.

It is not easy to describe the lasting impression which the deep undercurrent of esprit de corps in a famous regiment makes on a newly joined member, whether an officer or a recruit, and in a short while this gets under the skin and into the bones, leaving a permanent feeling of great pride, loyalty and security.

It was a strange coincidence that on the very day of our arrival in Bannu, a raiding gang of Mahsud[12] tribesmen from across the border had carried out an armed raid on a village well within India. Not being able to get back with their loot into their independent territory, under cover of darkness they had taken shelter in a cave below the cliff of a dry nullah bed.[13] A brave villager, taking his life in his hands, had followed the raiders and seen where they had gone to ground. Racing back to the nearest police post he gave the news, and within an hour a strong posse of Frontier Constabulary (FC) jawans[14] moved out and took up their position on the cliff overlooking the cave's mouth. The Mahsud gang was trapped and the leader knew it. Despite the jeers and taunts of his enemies he naturally refused to come out with his gang and shouted back abuse in his own dialect. The FC men also took no notice of the leader's suggestion that they should come along and get them. Frontier Constabulary men were all Pathans and anything but cowards, however they were not going to be such fools as to invite certain death by appearing at the mouth of that cave to be silhouetted against the morning light. It was seldom that such a golden opportunity came their way to get certain and easy revenge on the hated dushman.[15] With the safety catches off their rifles forward and their fingers itching and close to their triggers, they bided their time while a messenger was sent off to 'phone their sahib, Handy, who would know how to deal with such a situation'.

Within an hour he came chugging and bumping along in his Tin Lizzie (Ford). Following closely came a half section of a mountain battery on its large, beautifully groomed mules, each led by a gunner at a steady trot. The plan of action soon took shape, and the mountain gun came into action on the opposite bank of the nullah. The Frontier Constabulary party above the cave broke up into two groups moving to safe positions right and left of the cliff and were ready to open fire if any Mahsud emerged. The gun then fired half a dozen shells into the mouth of the cave which was soon enveloped in clouds of smoke and dust, but this did not force out any raider nor did a few further rounds. Perhaps all the raiders were dead or wounded, it was impossible to say, but the CO of the Constabulary was not taking any unnecessary risks to jeopardize the life of any of his men and he sent off to the nearest village for large bundles of straw and a couple of long bamboo poles. When these arrived the straw was dropped in front of the cave mouth and pushed in as far as possible with the poles.

All was now ready for the final act of the drama. The FC riflemen made certain that their weapons were ready and a few handfuls of burning straw were thrown down to mass in the cave's mouth. In a minute smoke and flames must have made the air within the cave unbearable. The raiders who, it was found later, had been sheltering in a side chamber of the cave and had clearly intended to hang on until nightfall when they would have a better chance of getting away, had to get out or be suffocated by the intense heat and fumes. The leader came out first, running towards the right, while the rest of the gang made off to the left. None of them had the slightest chance of escaping the hail of bullets which was directed against them and within a second or two all lay dead.

We heard the details of the above encounter from Handy, who came to our Mess for dinner on our next guest night. Of stocky build, with a mass of dark hair flaked with white, he had a quiet unassuming manner and no one meeting him for the first time casually would think that he was anything but just an average

13

officer serving on the Frontier. But, when in mess kit and wearing his miniatures, one would notice his Police Decoration and bars, and realize that here was no ordinary officer. If, after dinner and the wine had gone round two or three times, he could be persuaded to tell of some of his adventures and encounters with raiders, his narrative, reluctantly told, would make us young subalterns hold our breath in awe. Such a man was 'Handy' of the Police, and with Sir George R.K. and Sir John Donald,[16] was famous on the North-West Frontier of India in those days, famous from the Black Mountains in the north to Dera Ghazi Khan in the south.

But to return to the story of that particular raiding gang which met with deserved disaster just outside the cantonment of Bannu. At lunchtime we heard about it and the CO suggested that we go along with the Adjutant after lunch to the Bannu market square to see the result of the encounter.

On arriving at the bazaar market we had to elbow our way through a dense crowd until we got to the edge of the circle which the spectators had formed. We saw seven bodies lying sprawled on the ground, most of them faced upwards, all stripped bare except for their *partoogai* (loose-flowing pants). Seven Mahsuds lay there with unseeing eyeballs turned to the sky and half-open mouths, in and out of which swarmed disgusting looking blue-bottle flies. Small red circles on the bodies indicated the bullet marks. The obvious leader was a great bull of a man. Surely it had been he who had been the first to run out of the cave to the right, to draw the fire of the FC rifles. The youngest of the gang could not have been more than sixteen years of age and, I must admit, I felt a twinge of remorse as I looked at his strong but lightly built young body. Never again would that boy feel the wind rushing past his ears as he bounded from rock to rock down some mountain slope. And his mother, for even Mahsud raiders had mothers, who looked forward to the return of her brave young son from his first raid with his share of the spoils, would wait in vain, perhaps never knowing what had happened.

Our first day with our own 77th Regiment found us 'blooded'. An old friend of mine, who had served on the Frontier during the First World War, told me the following story:

We arrived at the village shortly after dawn, the Mahsud raiders had made off a few hours before we arrived. The women of the village were still screaming from fear and pain at the ghastly handling they had all received at the hands of the gang. The Mahsuds had torn and ripped the gold ornaments out of the noses and ears of the owners and in one case a woman's finger had been cut off to get a gold ring. Some of the men folk who had shown resistance had been shot out of hand and their bodies flung out on to the roadway while their dwellings were pillaged.

A true story and not the only such story I've heard. Sometimes a gang of raiders would remove a villager and hold him to ransom. If the money were not forthcoming a finger of the unfortunate would be delivered, somehow or other, with another demand. If this failed to produce the ransom the remainder of the hand would be sent along, somehow or other, accompanied by a last demand that the head of the victim would be delivered to the family if they failed to pay the money within the time limit. A Mahsud risks his life in every raid he takes part in or in any ambush, and to get what he wants he will show no consideration. In return he will expect none. A good rifle to him is his most precious possession, much more so than his wife. On the other hand the three chief causes of blood feuds amongst them are women, land and water disputes.[17]

His country is wild and cruel. In the eastern portion the fierce heat from March to October makes that part almost unbearable and uninhabitable, and except for a few who eke out an existence in cave dwellings, it remains deserted during those months. Further west near the Afghan border, the country rises rapidly to considerable heights in the mountains, and in this belt of country the cold for several months is severe. So the majority of the population lives in the narrow portion between these areas. Here they have their large fortified villages and their few miserable fields. But there is not enough cultivated land to go round and the average Mahsud is poor, very poor, as regards worldly goods but not in regard to arrogance. He is over-brimming with this characteristic.

A Mahsud prides himself on being a good rifle shot and being quick with his deadly razor-sharp dagger, on his fleetness in the mountains, his eagle-sharp eye, his disdain of danger and on his hardiness which enables him to exist for days on his reserve ration of a small bag of flour, on his intimate knowledge of the country and where every path, cave and spring of water can be found, and also on his eye for ground and his ability to plan a raid or ambush. His power of endurance is almost unbelievable for he can cover 40 miles in a day without turning a hair. In the years I write there were no schools or hospitals in their land and when a Mahsud took sick the normal treatment was 'sheep skin'. This cure for all ills consisted in slaughtering a sheep, removing the still warm skin, wrapping the patient in it and leaving him in it for days. Strangely enough this cure seemed to work quite often and was also used for a badly wounded man.

Fifty years ago the tribe had a very famous and influential leader by the name of Powinda. He was a religious man, a mullah, and lived in safety in the west, in a cave dwelling, inaccessible to our forces and immune from bombing attack. For many years his hold over the Mahsuds was paramount, with the result that the political authorities were sometimes able to come to reasonable terms through him with his tribe. However, after his death his son and successor, Faisal Din, was not able to wield the same power as the great mullah and the Maliks, or headmen of the Mahsuds, failed to prove that they had sufficient influence to curb more than those immediately under them. The hotheads of the clans remained unmanageable and continued to be thorns in the side of the British Raj. At heart, nearly every Mahsud is a hothead.

Tribal allowances were paid, in return for good behaviour, to this tribe, as well as to all other tribes on the Frontier across the border, but I do not think that much of this money ever found its way into the pockets of the poorer members of the community. As these had little or no land to subsist on their attention turned to raiding across the border into India. These incursions not only brought their rewards in the form of money, jewellery, cloth, grain and the odd rifle with precious ammunition, but also the excitement and adventure which is the lifeblood of most cross-border Pathans.

Living in a community in which 'baddi',[18] or blood feud, is a recognized part of tribal law, as a result of which sometimes whole family male members are killed off in turn, it follows that life tends to be cheap and of little consequence. From birth onwards a Mahsud youth grows up in a fierce atmosphere. From these facts perhaps some excuse emerges for the Mahsuds' savage tendencies.

To understand some of the problems that confront the Army when operating in Tribal Territory across the border, and the special kind of precautions these demand, I shall try to explain some points. Since pre-First World War times, conditions had advanced quite a lot and whereas, in days gone by, chivalry of a kind existed, was understood and honoured by both sides, this was fast disappearing and in fact had more or less completely disappeared by 1915. This was due, to a large extent, to the introduction on our side into Frontier warfare of new types of weapons which the tribesmen considered unfair and even barbarous, and which resulted in vengeful and bitter feelings on their part. Now without any declaration of Jihad, or Holy War, life in the border regions became unsafe. In the hills, any movement of personnel or convoy away from a camp or fort, and without proper escort or adequate protection, was liable to attack. Although sniping from distant hilltops which overlooked the route could not always be guarded against, ammunition with the tribesmen is never abundant and therefore greatly valued, and this sort of attack could never be but desultory and only of nuisance value. Continual vigilance was necessary both when moving in the valleys and when in picquets or on perimeter guard in camp, because at no time are troops immune from the danger of cunningly laid plots or '*chapaos*', or thieving entries into camps on dark nights. Every line of approach to the route to camp, a picquet or even a temporarily held hilltop should be suspect as being under the observation of some concealed tribesman, and if in his view one such way was unguarded then surely danger threatened. One of the most deadly sins of omission of a commander, whether he be a lance naik[19] in charge of a picquet,[20] or a unit commander responsible for a length of camp perimeter, is to fail to guard against the danger from a concealed approach to a point on his sector. He not only fails in his responsibility as regards the safety of his own men, but by his negligence jeopardizes the lives of others in the camp.

About 30 or 40 miles to the west, across the border in the Tribal Territory, there stands a strong fort, Miranshah, and alongside is a

17

small cantonment of huts. The fort is the headquarters of the South Waziristan Militia,[21] known to all on the Frontier as the Tochi Militia guarding the Tochi Valley. A couple of permanent Indian Army battalions occupy the hutted camp. This strong garrison was stationed there in those days because of the deteriorating relations between our government and Afghanistan which, it seemed, never failed to lose any opportunity of exciting the tribes to revolt against us, giving promises of support if they did.

It was not long before I was sent from Bannu up the Tochi to this little cantonment to be attached to one of the two companies of our battalion stationed there, and my training in trans-border operations commenced. My company commander was barely a year senior to me and therefore had little Frontier experience. However we had a really fine lot of Indian officers, afterwards referred to as VCOs, and it was from them that I learnt about most of the dangers to look out for.

A few weeks after arriving at Miranshah my turn came round to command the escort that always accompanies any convoy moving in the area. Every week a convoy of camels carrying rations, ammunition and baggage went up the Tochi route to posts situated further back in Mahsud and Wazir[22] territory. Motor vehicles were scarce in those days, the tracks were rough and unsuitable for them, and camel was found the best means of trans-porting goods. Each animal carries up to 400lb and, although he is a slow mover, he is capable of keeping up this rate of march for hours on end without tiring.

In the early morning, by the time we arrived with the escort, the camels had been loaded and were on the road outside the fort ready to move off. As is usual with camels, some of them were protesting loudly, but once we got moving they ceased their roaring and padded along silently with their long tread. To keep the convoy as short as possible, it proceeded in parallel lines of animals; even so it extended back about 200 yards. The camel men, one in charge of about four or five beasts, walked holding a long nose string at the head of his line. Each camel has a slit in his nose into which is fitted a wooden plug, and to this is tied the end of the nose string, about 10 feet long. The forward end of that string is tied to the tail of the camel in front, and so it is not difficult to calculate that a beast with its nose string takes up about seven yards of the track. If for some reason a camel stops, the one in front will pull out the wooden plug from the nose of the stationary animal and will be led along for some distance before this becomes known to the man in charge. The camels following the one which has halted will crowd round it. This mass of animals has then to be disentangled before the convoy can proceed. For this reason it is just as well that camels do not need to stop when they wish to urinate. The last animal (or vehicle) of every convoy has a red flag on a pole tied to its load. No portion of the convoy must be behind this flag. This is essential information for the picquets which occupy the protective positions on hills dominating the route, for these picquets cannot withdraw until the tail of the convoy as well as the close escorting troops are well and safely on their way. The posts and forts are responsible for putting up the route picquets ahead of the time the convoy is due to pass, while the escort of the convoy is to prevent any interference by enemy on any part of it in case of an attack having broken through the picquet line at some point.

Our first stop was at Boya post, not many miles from Miranshah. Even so I was glad to have it for I had found the slow trudging along at about two miles an hour most boring. After a night stop we continued on our march to Datta Khel, a large fort with a strong garrison of the Tochi Militia. Because of this post's strategic position and the long way it was from headquarters at Miranshah, a battalion officer was always stationed there in command. I was welcomed and fed like a king during my two days' halt there, and so enjoyed the change that I was loath to take my departure for our return trip. My host, the young Militia officer, recounted many yarns about the tribesmen, their wiles and plots in their attempts to procure arms, ammunition or loot, and the rough and tumble excitement of life in this fierce land of crags and black burnt rocks. He told me about these recalcitrant people who lived in caves, in strongly fortified villages and strong, high towers, whose one delight and ambition was the possession of a good British-made rifle with which he could slay an enemy at great range. His vivid description of encounters thrilled me and, when later on I was given a chance of transferring to one of these Frontier Corps units, I accepted with alacrity and as a result, landed myself with more excitement than I had bargained for.

In later years I realized that this was my lot and my destiny, and my share in the war. Many officers of my seniority, including my brother, had gone overseas to Mespot, Palestine and Persia to join their unit already there, or else had gone with them, whereas I saw no likelihood of seeing service overseas in the Battalion to which I subsequently found myself posted.

My chance came sooner than I expected, for after a month or two in Miranshah a couple of us were summoned down to HQ in Bannu, and ordered to pack up and join a new battalion of our group which was being raised in the Malakand.[23] At that time the Malakand was a peaceful one-battalion station. Officers were allowed to have their wives there, but as we were all bachelors it might just as well have been a no-family station, except that at weekends the officers invited their friends from the nearby stations at Mardan, Risalpur, Nowshera and Peshawar. With the band of our first Battalion, which had been left with us when they went overseas, we were well able to entertain our visiting friends.

During the few months I was with the 2nd Battalion Guides in the Malakand, I was able to finish with the two examinations for retention in the Army, and so when the opportunity came and officers were called for, there was nothing to hinder my applying for Militias. Before being accepted every officer had to be personally vetted by the Chief Commissioner of the province, in my case Sir George R.K., a famous Political Officer on the Frontier and one deeply respected by all the tribes, for there was nothing he did not know about their religion, customs and laws. To meet the Chief Commissioner I was directed to report at the charming little Militia station of Parachinar, up the Kurram valley beyond Kohat. To get there I had to go by railway beyond Kohat to the terminus at Thal, after which a good metalled road climbed up the gradient to Parachinar. I was highly honoured and in luck's way, for R.K. with his usual thoughtfulness and generosity sent his car down to meet me. It was an enormous touring car, pillar box red and with the exhaust note of a Brooklands racer. How I enjoyed that ride up from the heat of the plains to the cool air of the high plateau, where the open cantonment and head-quarters of the Kurram Militia are located. Nice bungalows and a luxurious Mess, all situated in the beautiful gardens, a peaceful people and a lovely invigorating climate all made Parachinar Kurram Militia a plum of a corps to get into. Here there was no exciting and dangerous soldiering, and life was as different as chalk is from cheese if compared with that found in the two militias in Waziristan. At any rate it was not for me. I was accepted for transfer and posted to the South Waziristan Militia, Wana, the most remote corps of the five: the Mohmand Militia, the Kurram Militia, the South and North Waziristan Militias and the Zhob Militia.

I returned to the Malakand to pack up and say goodbye to my friends there. I was not to see my regiment again for eight years.

To join my new unit I took the train again to Mari Undus, this time not for Bannu but for Tank. After crossing over the river to Kalabagh, where I had a meal, I caught the next train on the miniature railway. About halfway to Bannu and at a small junction, Laki Marwat, the Tank line branches off south. Laki boasts of a small refreshment room and as day trains arrive there at about lunchtime, I got down for the meal. The guard of the train had asked me a few stations back if I would like him to order lunch for me and so I found it ready, coloured soup, chicken cutlets (most probably goat) and burnt custard pudding. Many times in after years I had lunch at this station but I never found the menu to change. The cook, I felt, only knew how to prepare the two dishes. The soup couldn't be called a dish, as it was just coloured water.

Even in September the weather was dreadfully hot and the Paxine, which covered the seats in the compartment, was painful to sit on until the cooler temperature of a human posterior gradually made the position bearable. There were two electric fans in the carriage and they worked quite well, but their wire guards were loose and every now and then fouled the blades emitting a really fiendish rattle which precluded any idea of sleep. At every stop the passengers would swarm out of the compartments on either side of the track to escape from the torrid atmosphere which the fierce sun stoked up in them. As I had travelled on this line about a year before I had a good idea what to expect, although on that occasion most of the journey had been done during the night. This time I had provided myself with a couple of *chaguls*, canvas bags shaped like jugs for holding water, and when these were tied dangling outside the windows of the compartment, the wind playing on the damp exteriors caused evaporation and kept the water really cool. These water bags saved my life that day. I don't think I've ever consumed so much liquid in one day as I did on that trip. Ice was not available for us poor passengers, although a quantity is always sent down the line from both Bannu and Tank, but this is soon consumed by the railway staff at the different stations. Who can blame them for this?

On arriving at Tank station I lost no time in getting out of the train and into a tonga which took me to the *dak* bungalow on the far side of the town. Here I had respite and was able to rest in peace on a bed placed under a huge *phanka* pulled by a sweating coolie who, unfortunate chap, squatted on the verandah. If one were to doze off and wake up in a sweat it was because the coolie had also dozed off. Then, to go on to the verandah and poke him in the ribs with a stick was the best way to get the *phanka* flapping furiously again.

The *dak* bungalow *khansama*[24] knew all about the South Waziristan Militia and had met a lot of the officers serving there on their way up and down through Tank. He was a nice old man and, besides telling me a lot about the conditions prevailing in Waziristan, and also a few blood-curdling stories of murders and raids, he made arrangements with the mail tonga,[25] booking the front seat for me, for my onward journey on the morrow. My instructions were that I was to be at post Murtaza on that day so as to be ready to proceed on the following day with the convoy, which went up the Gomal river valley weekly.

That evening I found a most unwelcome visitor in my bedroom. As I walked out of the door of the bedroom on to the verandah I saw the black head and about two inches of neck of a large snake protruding from the edge of the matting that covered the floor of the room. Collecting a good stout stick from the chowkidar,[26] we returned to slay it but could find no trace of it, although I turned back the edge of the matting as far as I could. That night I slept with that vile serpent in the room but I was careful not to put a foot out of bed during the dark hours.

I was awake at five the next morning when the *khansama* arrived with hot toast and a pot of tea. About half an hour later there was blast from a bugle from away up the road and I was told that the tonga was on its way. Sure enough, His Majesty's mail arrived with a clatter and another note from the bugler. It swept into the compound and drew up smartly by the steps of the verandah where my kit was ready to be strapped on to the broad mudguards. Two spanking little ponies drew the tonga, one in the shafts and the second pulling on traces to the left. We were soon ready to start, but I was quite unprepared for the sudden hand-gallop at which the vehicle shot off and out of the gate, going roughly on one wheel, or so it seemed to me. I wondered whether this furious driving was just a flash in the pan done to impress the passengers and encourage them to part with a good tip at the end of the journey. But no, for I found that in more trips in after months that this kind of driving was usual. I was in front with the driver and the back seats were full. This meant that the assistant driver who blew on the old and tarnished bugle had to hang on with a precarious foothold to some parts of the *garry* which he had to feel for.

The little steeds took my fancy. They were strong, well fed and well groomed. The contractor who ran the mail service was surely a man who had an eye for horseflesh and was a lover of his animals. We kept going at a good speed and mile after mile of the well-kept metalled road flashed by under our wheels until, when approaching a small village, a series of piercing shrieks emitting from the instrument carried by the assistant made me look round and note with wonder how that individual maintained his insecure contact with the carriage, at the same time blowing with such gusto. That horrible noise was a warning signal for the fresh horses, already prepared for their morning chore, to be brought out to the roadside. We really charged down the last 200 yards as though the ponies were determined to demonstrate to us mere humans that they were by no means tired out. Coming to a sudden halt amidst a cloud of dust and small stones, and now wet with sweat, they were soon taken out of the way for the fresh ones to be brought in and harnessed. In little or no time we were on our journey again and, with the sun gaining strength, I was beginning to look forward to arriving at our stopping place.

It wasn't much later that we sighted Murtaza post in the distance and in about fifteen minutes arrived at the bungalow gate where we all unloaded. I was expected and met by the Indian officer who was in command of this, the lowest of the South Waziristan posts. Officers' rooms were inside the fort. This saved having to post extra guards on the house, were I to occupy it at night, and when I went into the gate I was glad to find that an officer had come down from Wana to meet me, escort me up and show me the ropes. In every large post there are officers' quarters and these are fully furnished and equipped with mosquito nets, cooking pots, crockery, cutlery and glass. But all stores and food had to be taken along by touring officers, whose servants accompanied them to do the cooking. The Militia officer who had kindly come down to meet me was one of the few Indian Civil Service men seconded for the duration of the war to serve in the Indian Army, and release officers for overseas. Four such officers had come to the South Waziristan Militia but one of them had unfortunately been killed at Sarwekai post, a few months previously, in a skirmish with Mahsuds.

After breakfast I was shown round the post and told how the different duties and responsibilities of this one were carried out. Murtaza was responsible for garrisoning, maintaining and periodically changing the men in two small block houses, Tomandu and Mudhassan, a few miles to the north-west, which were situated to guard a track that raiding gangs used and which passed over a low depression into the valley beyond. There was a well-known spring in the further of the two posts. This little fort, dangerously situated in the valley itself, was to deny this water to returning parties of plunderers. That afternoon, after an early lunch, the two of us officers, with a strong escort of our Militia soldiers, walked over the rough stony plain to inspect these two isolated towers. Accompanying us were a few camels carrying the replenishing rations for the garrisons, and also the kits of the men who would be relieving them. The two posts had been warned the day before by a runner that they were to be rationed and relieved, and so all was spick and span and ready for us. Within an hour or two we had looked over the posts, inspected the reserve water and rations, checked the ammunition and were on our way back to Murtaza, which we could see from the ridge where the nearer of the little posts was located. By five in the afternoon we were back, hot, tired and waiting for tea which was waiting for us.

Having completed our visit I was glad that it would never fall to my lot to be one of the garrison of those little forts, especially a member of the one in the valley. Overlooked, dominated by hills, a couple of Mahsud snipers could, if they wished, make life unbearable for the unfortunate garrison, bottling them up as one would insects. And were it ever the unhappy lot for them to be besieged, it would surely have taken not less than a brigade to extricate the garrisons. Only twice during my tour with the South Waziristan Militia did I visit those small posts. This was the first time, the last being in 1919 when evacuating South Waziristan and fleeing by night through the hills. Branching off from the main route, my small rear party called in on the way. That night it was early to bed so as to be up in good time the following day for our journey up the Gomal. From Murtaza the rough track leads towards a gap in the low range of the nearest Waziristan hills. On the far side of this we got our first glimpse of the Gomal River, which was crossed by the only bridge that spans it. Not very far from this stands, silhouetted against the sky, the little post of Spink, quite an impregnable though small fort, situated on a long narrow ridge. We were to pass by this post as it is not suitable for accommodating a convoy and is too short a march from Murtaza.

As we crossed the bridge to the right bank of the river, which flows broad, placidly and clear over a gravelly bed, a large party of Suleman Khel Powindahs[27] with their families and droves of camels and donkeys were coming up the ford close by, led by their chieftains riding horses, mostly Arabs. They looked a fine lot: big, tough-looking men carrying rifles or long sticks for driving their animals, cheery well-fed, red-faced women, some carrying their infants and others with new-born babies, riding quiet, well-mannered camels. Several happy boys and girls accompanied the caravan. Because their animals shied at the bridge the caravan was crossing the ford, not much more than three feet deep. The girls, quite unashamedly pulling their skirts up to their thighs, waded through with shrieks of laughter, casting bold glances at my companion and myself, perhaps the first Britishers or white faces some of them had ever seen.

Many of these nomads find their way to Australia where they barter some of their good camels and in return bring back Australian walers, fine big horses, which they sell at enormous profit on their return to Afghanistan. Some of them have been known to bring back Australian wives and also Australian accents.

Before they are allowed entry into India all their rifles and weapons have to be deposited in Murtaza with a political official responsible for passing them through. They have their weapons with them during their passage through Waziristan to ensure safe way through this trouble area. They also engage paid *badraggas* (safe conduct locals). But being well-armed and good fighters, they themselves are able to give a good account of themselves if attacked, which sometimes happened. However the Wazirs and Mahsuds were well aware that any attack made by them would surely bring retribution, delayed though it may be for a few months, on their villages from the Afghan side of the Durand Line.

These Powindah caravans flowed down into India through other passes besides this Gomal route. I have seen them passing through the Tochi Valley and also the Khyber defile. Coming chiefly for trade they also avoid the severe winter cold of their own country, returning when the plains of Hindustan got too hot for their families.

A personal escort of seven or more mounted infantry men was always detailed to accompany any officer touring in Waziristan to deter the odd Mahsud or Tarir from lying up close to the route and taking an easy shot at a British officer as he rode past. This arrangement also enabled officers to have breakfast at a comfortable hour and then, riding along at a trot, catch up with the convoy about halfway to the next post.

The South Waziristan Militia kept several *maris* (riding camels) and two of these were always allotted to each touring officer. One carried his bedding roll and a few odds and ends, and the other took the officer's servant and lunch for his arrival at the next post. A *mari* had its own driver who was responsible for just one animal. He rode in the front of the two comfortable seats and was unarmed. These trotting camels can keep up a good pace and this meant that the servant could be at the next post in good time to have lunch ready for his sahib on his arrival. Besides the two *maris*, two donkeys also went along on any lengthy tour. Each of these strong little beasts carried two *yakdans*,[28] which are packed with a sufficient quantity of stores, vegetables and fruit to last the tour. They are switched along by an unarmed follower and stay with the convoy. So it can be appreciated that every tour in South Waziristan in those days was quite a complicated venture, and not like touring in other Militia areas where most of it could be done by car. Alternately trotting and walking our horses, we completed our ride to the next post, Nili Kach, in less than four hours, well before lunchtime and even before the *maris* caught up with us and our servants. The post is perched on an isolated knoll overlooking a plain. Well built and easy to defend, it had good accommodation for all and, although the midday temperature was high, this was considerably less than that experienced in Tank and Murtaza. Also, the nights are pleasantly cool.

After lunch and a short rest my companion suggested that we go out for a couple of hours' shoot. Since the early age of ten I've been a keen shikari so naturally I was ready in a few minutes. Not far to the west of the post quite a considerable area of the plain is low lying, damp and covered with tall elephant grass. This is the only place in Waziristan where I have come across this type of ground. Taking an armed covering party of a dozen men and a few beaters, we moved through the tall grass slowly. It was so thick underneath that we had almost to fight our way forward. However we had our reward in the shape of three or four partridge plus a quail or two. These 'black' are attractive birds, slightly larger than a grey partridge but considerably easier to shoot, for they rise with a loud warning squawk perpendicularly for about 10 feet before flying away parallel to the ground. The only hope of finding a shot bird in this thick grass was to drop it dead. A runner was quite impossible to recover. This grass-covered plain is reputed to hold wild pig, but we did not see any. In any case, it would not have been good shooting one as our Pathan militiamen were all Mohammedans, for whom pigs are unclean and untouchable. For dinner that night we had a 'black' apiece – white, dry and not very interesting to consume. Instead of having them roasted we should have had them stewed, with lots of vegetables. The spotted soft feathers from under the wings of a 'black' are carefully plucked for slipping under the ribbon of a shikari's felt hat, as we do with the beautifully curled, dark-green tail feathers of a drake mallard.

The next day we made for Khajuri post, not a very long march but a very nasty one, including a passage through a rough and tumble of low mud hills and a long, deep ravine. This dreadful, broken-up bit of Waziristan is called the Gularree. It is quite uninhabited, is destitute of scrub and grass, and the only liquid I ever saw there is a sulphur spring which envenomed the already overpowering oppressive air that always seems to hang heavily in that cauldron. It seemed to invite the *chapoas*, and in fact a battle had been fought there not many months previously between Mahsuds and the picqueting troops out from Nili and Khajuri. The Mahsuds, who had taken up positions on several knolls from which they could fire on the areas which the picqueting troops were sometimes known to take up, opened fire simultaneously, up and down the ravine, and even tried a rush or two. However their scheme failed, for the Khattak Pathans they were up against, having no love for the Wazirs and Mahsuds, fought back with great courage, thereby nullifying the initial advantage the enemy had gained by their surprise tactics.

Khajuri post is also situated on a large plain, some distance from where the track emerges from the hills. The Gomal flows by a few hundred yards to the north and there is very little opportunity for enemy to give trouble. Because of the easy terrain a keen fisherman can indulge to his heart's content in his favourite sport, as numerous and fine fish are in the river.

From a little west of Nili to Khajuri, the convoy route is a good distance from the gorge which restricts the Gomal and it is not visible until the track approaches the Khajuri plateau several miles further on. In early 1919, a road was being constructed by Mahsud labour under the supervision of a British engineer, and on a tour through the Gomal posts I met him at Khajuri. When he suggested that I go down the new road he was making and meet my convoy further down at Nili, I was happy to agree, for not only had I a hatred of the Gularee, which to me seemed to smell of death, but I was intrigued by the clearer waters of the Gomal and the hidden way it disappeared into a steep-sided gap, cut centuries past, through a solid mountain. The mouth of this gorge is called Adam Kok by the locals and the Gomal, which is broad and easily fordable opposite Khajuri, narrows considerably and flows deep, dark and silently once it gets to the Kok. What huge deep pools there are and what monster mahseer[29] they must hold!

That British road-building expert carried his life in his hands, working with Mahsud labour and being protected by Mahsud *badraggas* – the only reason for his safety was that those Mahsuds were well paid for the work they were doing and the protection they guaranteed. All I can say is that I would have hated that lonely and dangerous job.

A few miles west of Khajuri, the River Zhob, flowing northwards from Fort Sandeman, joins forces with the Gomal and, when in spate, comes down with a rush of red mess of thickly muddied water, staining the usually clear waters of the Gomal and killing off large numbers of fish which the flood deposits on the banks. When in spate the route from Khajuri to Wana is closed, for the ford crosses the combined waters of both rivers just above the post. However, the post has good accommodation and there is no hardship in having to spend a few nights and days there. In fact, the engineer I met had made Khajuri his headquarters for this reason and also, of course, because he always had a chance of meeting the odd touring British officer from Wana.

Above Khajuri the country opens up, except for a few lowish spurs so that protecting the convoy track on to Tanai presents a few problems for the picqueting troops. Sometimes a party would go through with only mounted infantry who were well versed in the procedure of occupying low hills, rapidly withdrawing and galloping forward again to take the next dangerous spur. However, this sort of movement was carried out as an exception and never as a rule.

The going is good and in less than three hours' riding we were at Tanai and, for the first time we saw cultivated hills and crops. A few hamlets are in this area and the odd Wazir can be seen tending his field or winnowing his grain. The country is more attractive and the air is cool, there is fairly good shooting of a rough kind to be had and I always enjoyed a day or two in this nice little post.

The fields of wheat extend to the low spurs which come down to the Tanai plain and along the edges of these cultivated areas. The little, light brown, extremely shy sisi can be found in coveys of about a dozen. If you are after these small hill partridge on the level and fail to get your birds with the first two barrels, then you must be prepared for really energetic and rough scrambling up the hills to which they invariably fly when disturbed. If you continue after them they seem always to be ahead and just out of range. Tantalizing to bag, there is, nevertheless, great satisfaction in dropping one on a hillside. But never imagine that you can get a right and left when on a hill. I have never achieved this nor have I ever seen it done. Shooting snipe is child's play to shooting sisi on a hill.

During the early autumn months when the crops are high, quail come in their hundreds on their way down into India where they are netted. The strong males, often painted dark red or blue, are sold to be trained to fight, while the rest are sold for the pot. The Pathan is very keen on training and fighting these pugnacious little cock birds and many rupees change hands in betting and backing. I have often joined the crowd of spectators making a ring round the two small contestants. Before the two birds are let loose at each other the handlers irritate their little heroes by tapping their heads and beaks with a finger. The fight is fast and furious during the short while it lasts until one of the fighters, having had enough, rushes round and round the close ring of jeering and applauding people, trying to escape the ferocious peckings of the victor. A quail will never become tame like a grey partridge, which will follow its master like a dog.

Walking up and shooting these fat little birds requires little marksmanship and is not much fun, for they won't rise until the guns are almost on them, and then fly off in a straight line, giving an easy shot. But to eat stewed or on toast, they are as succulent and tender as snipe, even more so.

I greatly enjoyed my first day at Tanai. The weather was wonderful after the plains of India and my friend and I had a successful afternoon with shikar. The British officers' quarters were found to have several library books and also a sizeable stack of old but most interesting copies of illustrated English weeklies: *Illustrated London News*, *Sphere*, *Tatler* and *Field*. All these were bound in good thick volumes and, although more than ten years old were still in perfect condition.

The following morning, so as to be in Wana, our HQ, early, we had breakfast at seven and rode off, catching up the convoy as it arrived at the meeting place of the picqueting troops from west and east. A few miles after leaving Tanai and passing through a low gap in the hills, we descended into the Wana Toi valley. The clear little bubbling stream rises in the Wana plain and flows a few miles, swinging south to join the Gomal above Khajuri post.

Between the low pass and Wana the route is protected by a small blockhouse situated by the stream and looking up a broad re-entrant, which is a danger spot as it leads into Mahsud-cum-Wazir territory to the north. This post is Karab Kot, manned by about twenty men, who have an easy and pleasant tour of a fortnight before being changed.

Continuing up the Toi, crossing and re-crossing the stream, we eventually arrived at the opening of the valley onto the Wana plateau which, once we had climbed up out of the nullah bed, stretched before our eyes. Less than a mile away was our destination, Wana post. Our ponies knew where they were and needed no encouragement to complete the distance at a steady canter.

[Editor's note: Cumming spent two years in Wana cantonment, which was established in the late nineteenth century. Until the British departed India in 1947, the Regular Army and the native levies were engaged in almost constant warfare with the fierce tribes of Waziristan. At the outbreak of a fully fledged insurgency in the 1930s, the British had 18,000 troops in and around Waziristan, with Wana being used as the forward headquarters and airbase. Wana today remains in the eye of a storm because of the embedded presence of foreigners who have affiliated them-selves with the Taliban-aligned Wazirs of the Wana plain and others in the area. Osama bin Laden is believed to be holing up in the mountains north-west of Wana under the protection of the tribes. The Pakistan Armed Forces have been conducting armed operations against Al Qaeda and Taliban militants since August 2003, under enormous pressure from the US-led occupation forces in Afghanistan.

In Cumming's day, the South Waziristan Militia (rechristened 'Scouts'), was one of several native levies, later collectively known as the Frontier Corps, inspired by the Viceroy, Lord Curzon, who withdrew the Army from the border tribal region. Curzon considered the system he inherited – under which the Government of the Punjab took responsibility for tribal policy and all decisions had to be channelled through Lahore before reaching the Viceroy's attention – as dangerously detached from the reality of Frontier life. The Frontier Corps' headquarters were permanently shifted two years after Partition to the imposing hilltop Bala Hissar fortress that towers over the main road leading into Peshawar. The Brigadier in command of the Frontier Corps holds jurisdiction over a huge swathe of territory from the Karakoram range at the northern extreme of the Frontier to the Mekran coast, 2,500 miles to the south. In Curzon's own words, the objective was the 'withdrawal of British forces from advanced positions, employment of tribal forces in defence of tribal country, concentration of British forces in British territory as a safeguard and a support, improvement of communications in the rear'. The irregular forces raised to guard the Frontier adopted the names of Militia, Scouts and Rifles. There are subtle distinctions between the three types of corps. Apart from the proper Frontier Forces, the Government created Khassadars as local police at the disposal of the political agents in the several tribal agencies. The militias were and still remain support units for the armed forces, whose recruits are Pathan tribesmen. Most of these militia units gradually adopted the title of Scouts, which more accurately describes their role as gathering information on tribal affairs and protecting troop movements through hostile territory by manning picquets and guarding the roads. The title of Rifles was used to distinguish Indian Army regiments that carried lighter equipment and moved faster over the Frontier's hilly terrain than heavy infantry units.

The fledgling RAF first came into action on the North-West Frontier in raids against the tribesmen during localized disturbances in Baluchistan and Waziristan, in 1916–17. Aerial bombardment was a tactic that the Pathans considered 'unsporting', yet the RAF in India came to play a key role in policing the North-West Frontier Province. With the outbreak of the Third Afghan War in 1919, the RAF was often in the forefront of dealing with incursions by Afghan militants or raids by local tribesmen, as an alternative to marching a punitive column into the troubled district. The Air Staff argued that the RAF could replace these costly military expeditions. Aircraft could strike swiftly and cheaply into the mountains, with comparatively little risk to the pilots.]

Chapter 2

War Clouds over Waziristan

And now, for me began a most happy and enjoyable period of nearly two years, just the sort of life a young and active man could hope for. We were a happy family and I cannot remember hearing of any quarrel amongst the officers, of whom there were about ten, including the Political Agent, a British engineer and our doctor. Of course two or three of them were usually away on short leave or inspection duty of posts. However, it was very seldom that a bridge four could not be made up after dinner. In fact, our isolated little world at that time was at peace and in rest from outside worries. The Mess was most comfortable and complete in every respect. In front of the Mess we had beautiful green lawns and flower beds, and the officers' quarters were spacious and fully furnished and equipped. We had first-class vegetable and fruit gardens, our own dairy and herd of cows, our own flock of sheep, our own bakery and, in the Mess store, an abundance of good tinned stores of all kinds which we indented upon before going on tour.

Office work, of which there was very little, was looked after by the CO, the Adjutant and the Quartermaster, assisted by a most efficient head clerk and office staff. Correspondence between posts and instructions regarding convoys and road openings were done in the vernacular by writers, who wrote the instructions on thick gaol-made paper. These letters were called *parwanas* and, after being read over to an officer, had to be initialled by him. A telegraph line ran from Wana down through the Gomal posts but, as far as I can remember, as often as not this was out of order.

The locals had an insatiable appetite for the 8-inch soft metal standards on which are fixed the white porcelain insulators carrying the wires. Each telegraph pole held two of these insulators, and their metal standards were ideal for shaping into the sharp pointed daggers which every local tribesman carried. These weapons are usually most beautifully engraved and have bone or ivory handles so shaped that the hand fits perfectly. Most Mahsuds wear their dagger slipped into their shirts behind their necks with the handle protruding a few inches. From this position it doesn't take a second for an expert to bring the deadly weapon into action.

In Wana there was always morning parade to get us up early and into uniform. This kept one occupied for an hour and a half and I never found this boring, for we trained our own recruits to fill up vacancies in the lower ranks. Our recruits were always lads of about eighteen, brought from their land by our men and Indian officers returning from leave. In this way we got reliable men vouched for by their serving relatives and, I may say, there was never any difficulty in keeping the Corps up to strength. Only Pathans were enlisted in Frontier militias and in the South Waziristan Militia we took several different classes: Khattaks, Afridis, Bangash, Yusafzais and, to please the political authorities, about fifty Wazirs. All these Pathans spoke the Pushtu language, but their dialects differed, in some cases quite considerably.

The men were armed with single-loading Lee Enfield .303 long rifles, very accurate and reliable weapons. Each man carried a brown leather bandolier with pouches to hold fifty rounds of Mark VI ammunition. This bandolier was slung over one shoulder and across the chest. When out on road protection duty or on *gasht*[1] the men wore *partogai*, long, loose trousers and a shirt, both made from *mazrie* cloth, a light grey-coloured material, hard wearing and ideal for the country we worked in. The dark-grey and black rock of those hills made a wearer almost invisible at anything above short range. A felt-covered water bottle and a light haversack for food, and first-aid pack completed a soldier's equipment. All Pathans, for footwear, prefer wearing sandals to boots, as the former are much lighter and also more flexible. These *chaplies*,[2] for hill work, are incomparable. All officers also wore this type of footwear and I became so accustomed to the *chapli* that I continued to use them all through my service, and still do.

35

During the autumn and winter months, when peace reigned on the Wana plain, all the British officers would go forth on Saturdays or Sundays on organized shoots, sometimes after chickor, sometimes after sisi, quail, snipe or tiloor.[3] To the south of our post was a large mud-covered plain sparsely covered with small shrub, and here tiloor could often be seen feeding. These handsome birds stand about two feet high and their plumage is a most attractive light drab, but when in their leisurely flight they exhibit a lot of white. It is not only difficult but almost impossible to approach within scatter-gun range of these shy birds. They almost always seem to have one bird doing sentry-go while his friends feed, and his eye is never shut to approaching danger. Many times we chased after these elusive bustard but only on one occasion did we succeed in bringing back a bird and that was the result of a fluke. At about 80 yards' range one of our party loosed off his piece at a driven bird and one single pellet found a vital spot. It was large enough for all of us to have a goodish portion and was a change from our normal shikar diet, however the eating thereof was to me nothing to write home about.

One day on a sisi shoot along the slope of Shisha picquet hill, which flanked the Toi, our line of guns came to a halt when a small white terrier belonging to one of the guns began barking furiously. It had found a large iguana half-submerged in a flooded field. This creature was the largest one of that kind I have ever come across for, from head to tail, it must have measured quite 3½ feet. The white yapping bitch was having fun tantalizing the hideous creature, which had by now climbed out of the water and was on a dry bank. Foolishly and incautiously, the dog approached too close to the hissing reptile. Some of us gathered round to watch the strange encounter that was going on and to intervene if necessary. However, the result not only came quicker than expected but proclaimed the unexpected victor, the iguana. With a lightning stroke, which was too swift for the eye to follow, the tail of the creature switched round suddenly, landing a tremendous blow on the yapping face. Yelping instead of yapping, and with her tail hidden between her legs, she ran to her master for protection, while the spectators scoffed at her discomfiture and the iguana, in peace, enjoyed his victory.

On another occasion when out on a shoot, my attention was drawn to a large viper which was curled up in a small shrub. Ever since my boyhood I have had a hatred of snakes and always endeavour to slay any poisonous one I come across. This I can usually tell for my father, who for many years was the Honourable Secretary of the Quetta McMahon Museum, had taught me a lot about birds, animals and reptiles that are to be found on the North-West Frontier of India. This viper had a broad flat head, thin neck, strong thickish body and short, abruptly terminated tail. It looked like an echis[4] for it had a cross mark on its forehead, but I was not going too close until I had despatched it. Borrowing my orderly's bayonet I slashed at its head, decapitating it within about an inch or two of its neck. Its head continued to make a hissing noise and, when I put the point of the bayonet near its mouth its great jaws closed upon it in a flash and like a vice it held on. The horrible venomous creature had fangs more than half an inch long.

Our favourite shoot was called the *Dhana* and we did this two or three times in the winter months, leaving a good period in between shoots so as not to scare the birds too much. It had its name from a long flat valley between a *warsak*, or spur and the high Marwati mountains, which lay to the north-west. This flat plain is the only area I know of where chikoor can be shot without having to scale up and down a hillside. Besides these beautiful birds this shoot also invariably produced hare, sisi, quail and a few grey partridge. Forming a long line of beaters and guns we would move slowly along and the birds, although sometimes rising in coveys, would often get up singly. Our total bag for the day would never be less than thirty and on a good day would count up to sixty. While the shoot was on, our Mess servants, having come out on three or four *maris*, would have prepared a picnic lunch for the shikaris. With great pleasure we all looked forward to the next *Dhana* outing.

The local Wazirs never liked going up this valley, at the head of which they had a few largish villages. We therefore never gave out ahead that a shoot would be on there on any given day. This would have invited trouble. I recollect that on one occasion we found that a series of sangars had been built and camouflaged on the long Azam Warsak ridge in anticipation by the locals that we would be going out on a certain day. Actually, we had intended to shoot the *Dhana* on that day and somehow or other the information had leaked out, but for some other reason that shoot had been postponed at the last minute, and the Wana Wazirs' idea of shikar misfired. This incident left us in no doubt as to the true feelings of the locals towards the South Waziristan Militia and it was an urgent reminder for us officers that in Waziristan, when moving about away from post or camp, safety precautions should never be slackened.

At a certain season in the year, usually during a full moon in late autumn, when touring in the Gomal valley, it would be one's good fortune to see the migration of thousands upon thousands of waterfowl, mostly mallard, teal, widgeon, pintail and geese. Their lines, which follow one after the other in endless procession, extend on either side of the valley until their ends are out of sight. They always fly high and above the river, I suppose in case some tired bird or old and sick parent should have to leave its line and alight for rest and food. I wondered how many hundreds of miles they accomplish in a single flight, where they come from after breeding and what part of India they are bound for. They leave India in the spring before the weather gets too hot, but I have never had the chance of seeing them on their return journey.

The Commanding Officer was good enough to arrange for me the purchase of a sturdy chestnut bobtail nag, a really first-class little beast and the best pony I've ever had. He didn't bite, kick or trip and was sound as a bell. His arrival in the lines caused a flutter amongst the MI (mounted infantry) for my little moke was entire. So much confusion, jealousy and disorder did his presence cause that the South Waziristan Militia vet was called in to perform the necessary operation. How well I remember his dejected countenance when I went to see him one morning. When I enquired 'Why?' my syce's[5] reply was, 'Colonel Sahib *ka hukum* (has so commanded).' I had not been told beforehand what was coming to my fat steed and I felt very sorry for him. However, in a week he was his cheery little self again, searching with his velvet lips in my shirt pockets for a lump of *gur*,[6] which he felt for sure would be there.

When my turn came round to go on my first tour it was my privilege to be accompanied by an officer, a very senior Indian

Civil Service officer, who had given up his job of Commissioner of a district in India to see service on the Frontier. He was indeed one of the old school, severe and commanding in appearance, leaving one in little doubt that, when serving in his civilian capacity he ruled his district with a rod of iron. But into his steely blue eyes, which usually glared fiercely from under shaggy brown eyebrows, there sometimes stole a softness which gave an indication that his heart was not all stone. This officer, whose name was Cotton, was a noted sportsman and a noted member of a famous pig-sticking club. What wonderful stories he used to tell me of some of his exciting encounters with wild boar. He was also a good shot with a scatter-gun and many a tip he passed on to me during shots and excursions, on which we were together. The tour on which he accompanied me was to a fort, Sarwekai, which is located on the border of Mahsud country. It was this large and strong post that was allotted to me specially, for keeping under supervision during my first two years in the South Waziristan Militia. Although this information was never passed on to me officially I sensed it from the beginning, because of the many times I was sent there on inspection duty. My intuition turned out to be correct.

To get there one rode off back towards Tanai, escorted by a strong posse of Mounted Infantry, although day picquets were also out on the main heights. The part of the country, once we had left Wana, the Toi valley and through which one had to ride, could never be considered even slightly friendly. It was too close to Mahsud land for that. Also the broken nature of the ground, large areas of which were covered in *gurguri*[7] bushes and further on in very thick scrub, necessitated special precautions. Taking a rocky track to the left, our party passed through a gap in the ridge named Gurguri after an edible blackberry bearing bush that grew there in abundance. A few miles further on, through a low valley picqueted by men out from Tanai, we came to the cross tracks, Tanai Sarwekai-Wana Sarwekai. Here, sticking out of the mud plain were two or three huge coal-black rocks, Tora Tiga, a good halting place for a few minutes to pass the time of day with the Indian officer out with the Tanai troops.

The going was good for the next few miles and our riding party would catch up with and pass the small convoy of camels and donkeys. In a little while we came within sight of Mudijan, a long high ridge debouching into the Mudijan plain, from which a post on the ridge gets its name. This little isolated blockhouse overlooks a spring at the foot of the ridge, and as this is the only water to be found for miles around, the post's importance was considerable, denying to raiding gangs not only an obvious rendezvous but also the high ground which we had to hold for convoy protection duties. I confess I never liked this cramped small post, far from friends and in a hostile locality where, to move about without the walls and without precautionary measures was asking for trouble. Only on road-opening days was it safe to move far from the post, because then strong parties from Tanai and Sarwekai were out and coming towards Madijan. The only good point about it was that a strong cool breeze always blew across the ridge. We dismounted at the foot of the ridge to give our horses a breather and leading them by the reins trudged up the long slope until, gaining the walls, we sat there and enjoyed the extensive view and the cool breeze, while our orderlies and the MI men loosed the girths of the horses.

My companion, taking an enormous pipe out of his bush shirt pocket proceeded to fill it to capacity and, lighting it, leant back against the wall. By this I realized that we would not be on our way again until that pipe bowl was exhausted. In a minute he explained: the four *maris* had only half an hour previously passed through so it was no good hurrying, as it would have meant a wait for our lunch to get prepared. I was in no hurry. It was pleasant sitting, resting and letting the cool wind blow through my shirt, and my friend was enjoying his pipe, which was making a noise like a hubble-bubble (an Indian water pipe).

We eventually started off to complete the last leg of the trip, and the country got more and more forbidding. Scrub and dwarf palm spread thickly over the small plains and low valleys, and high rocky hills rose on either side of the track, but at quite a distance from it. Too far and dangerous to picquet with small groups but not too distant for sniping, had any Mahsud wished to resort to this irritating form of attack.

Game there is in fair abundance: chickor, grey, black and sisi, but by this time we were set out for Sarwekai, a good lunch and a rest. Rounding the last high spur, which came right down to the track, we got our first view of the fort set high up on a long pinkish ridge and looking enormous against the sky. We broke into a trot, keeping it up until we arrived at the bottom of the narrow road leading to the gates. We were met by a couple of Indian officers and after many 'Mastare mashee' and 'Khawar mashee'[8] we walked up to the post and entered the huge iron gates. A strong quarter guard had fallen in and presented arms as we passed through, and my companion stood and took the salute as stiffly as would a general officer commanding an army. Actually, when in his own district a commissioner ranks above a major general. At the far end of the post the officers' quarters and Mess were upstairs and so looked down on the inside of the area. We climbed the stairs and were pleased to find our lunch waiting to be consumed by us two hungry officers. My friend, although in the Army as a captain, was still drawing his enormous civilian pay. Being a bachelor with no worry about his pension, he spent lavishly and we fed on the very choicest of tinned foods.

When he left his district to join the South Waziristan Militia he had brought along two of his best mounts. One was a huge coal-black horse with long flowing tail and mane. One eye had a fierce glint and the other was wall-eyed, damaged in an encounter. This formidable-looking warhorse left one with the impression that its own obvious courage matched the confidence of its intrepid and experienced master and that in any encounter, with even the fiercest of boars, it would keep unswervingly on the charging course set by his rider, with the sure instinct that the spear would put an end to their enemy before its tusk could rip open his belly with a deadly slicing jab.

My friend's other steed, a 16-hand, really beautiful golden chestnut mare with soft, brown eyes and a gorgeous mane and tail, was clearly his favoured one. To see the two of them in close fellowship, cheeks rubbing and the arm of the tall, austere man encircling the neck of his best friend, it was easy to see that his main affections were directed towards his horses.

On this trip he rode the mare, holding in his right hand one of his long pig-sticking spears. Not that there was the slightest chance of being greeted by a boar, but just to keep in touch with and not lose the feel of his favourite but deadly weapon.

After lunch and a rest for two hours we took a walk round the post. High, well built and impregnable from attack which any-sized Mahsud *lashkar*[9] would ever dare to make, it was further guarded by two broad, barbed-wire entanglements. However, it had a weak spot. Its water supply was not secure and, of course, water is the most vital of all necessities. There was a spring that issued out at the foot of the ridge, below the fort from where the road started up towards the main gate. A cement-lined pool collected the water which was then taken up to the large water tanks in the post. A couple of bullocks were employed in this job, each carrying two large-size *pakhals*.[10] Thus the tanks in the post were always kept filled and, in an emergency, would last a couple of months. For a long siege this, of course, would not be enough and the present arrangement had proved vulnerable. A few months before I came and after a bloody encounter with Mahsuds not far from the post, the enemy had stuffed the dead body of one of our men through the opening of the concrete wall into the pool, contaminating it. The whole structure had to be broken down and rebuilt, and although this incident had fully demonstrated the vulnerability of the arrangement, the authorities had not sanctioned the building of a small covered-in tower over the actual pool. This would have solved the difficulty and the worries of the post commander. A deep communication trench protected by high parapets zigzagging down the slope would have enabled men to bring up water daily. As it was, eighteen months later, when encouraged by Afghanistan, the whole Frontier burst into flames and we had to evacuate this strategically invaluable fort, occupying a position of threat on the south flank of the Mahsuds, the most refractory and recalcitrant of all the Frontier tribes, and always a thorn in the flesh of the British Raj.

That night it was early to bed for a tired-out body and with the knowledge that the next morning would demand my presence on the parade ground. My companion, who took little interest in squad drill and rifle exercises, would inspect the stables and animal lines. Sarwekai, situated well above 3,000 feet had quite a cold nip in the air at six-thirty in the morning. But after doubling round the parade ground a couple of times the troops were warm enough to carry on with normal drill in comfort. Once the sun was well up in the blue sky the outside temperature rose rapidly and any excessive exercise was likely to make one sweat profusely, even in that dry atmosphere in the late autumn.

After breakfast the following morning we went through the usual procedure of inspecting a post and filling in the form which had to be given in at the office of the Commanding Officer to look at and issue any orders on: arms and ammunition, treasure chest and cash balance, barracks, men's kits, hospital, ration store, water tanks, outside protective wire, animals, their lines and feeds and, last of all a durbar.[11] This last was held in the courtyard of the post. The Indian officers and ourselves sat in a semicircle on chairs, and anyone else who wanted to look on came and sat on the ground, completing the circle, except for a gap in the circle opposite to where we sat. The main idea of having durbar is to give any individual of the unit an opportunity to make a complaint or put forward a petition. The presiding officer then makes a decision on any points. In addition to this any lower rank man considered to have made a misdemeanour would be brought up before the durbar, escorted by his section commander or the senior man of his class. The culprit's misdeed would be stated, witnesses produced, the man's conduct sheet considered and sentence passed by the senior officer present. On the whole there was very little serious crime in the South Waziristan Militia. I think that this was due to the fact that the Commandant had very strong powers: he could give a man three months' rigorous imprisonment and dismissal without referring to higher authority. The real sting of such a punishment did not end there. The man's family would soon come to hear about it and later the tribe or sub-tribe would have some rough words to pass on the family concerned for the disgrace brought on them as a whole. For this reason heavy sentences were sparingly given.

The following morning we were free to have a shoot. The area that we had decided to beat over was the dwarf-covered plain just south of the post. This bit of the country gave me the impression that at some time, thousands of years ago, water covered this basin or cup, being held up by the high Sarwekai ridge, until one day the weight of the lake broke the barrier, leaving the mud-covered basin, ideal soil for the present vegetation it supported so luxuriously. The drainage was from south to north towards the ridge our post was on, and this ridge ended abruptly in a steep rocky sided gorge, which I imagine was the outlet forced by the water.

After putting out a couple of picquets, we went to the south edge of the basin and, making a long line with a dozen armed beaters, we swept through the scrub, back towards the post. Our plan was well rewarded for we collected a good mixed bag of grey, black, the odd quail and a couple of hare. The orderlies halaled (cut the throat) of the two hares as soon as they were picked up, knowing that these were always given to them and the beaters as their share of the spoil. Their Mohammedan religion demands that 'ye shall not eat the blood thereof'. After shooting the basin we moved down the spur hoping to pick up a sisi and, on arriving at the gorge, a chickoor. We were lucky in bagging a couple of sisi but were too late to find the chickoor at the gorge. They had watered and gone up into the rocks where we could hear them calling. It was warming up now and as partridge, both grey and black, show a marked tendency to sit tight and not rise when the air gathers heat, we called it a day and returned for a hearty breakfast.

Two out-of-date but nevertheless efficient 2.5-inch mountain guns were included in the permanent defence arrangements of this fort. This section of old screw guns was still good for firing many hundreds of rounds and in the post there were ample reserves of shells, illuminating shells and powder. A specially trained section of Militia personnel manned these muzzle-loading pieces, the barrels of which, when out of action were in two pieces. These two pieces had to be screwed together, hence the name for this type of artillery. When used as mobile mountain guns three or four strong mules were required to carry each gun, which broke up into several bits, but our section of guns was only used as garrison artillery and never left the post.

To fire a gun a small bag of powder was rammed down the muzzle until it reached the breech. A shell was then pushed down until it touched the bag of powder. To ignite the powder a detonator was used and this was pushed into a vent situated above the breech. To explode the detonator onto the powder a small projection on the end of the detonator had to be jerked out with the help of a lanyard. It all sounded rather complicated but with a well-trained crew it did not take more than a few seconds to fire, reload and fire again.

While with my regiment in the Malakand I had attended a machine-gun course in Ahmednagar. In those days each battalion had a section of Maxim machine guns, very efficient but very heavy, later replaced by the beautiful Vickers guns. Having learnt a little about trajectory, indirect fire, range taking and fire orders, I took a special interest in these artillery pieces. In fact I attached myself, in an honorary capacity, to the section. Ever since I was a lad of ten or so I had had a gun of my own, from a Daisy air gun through the range of BSA air guns, .22 rifle, .440 shotgun and a DB 12-bore. Therefore it was only natural that I should be attached to these weapons. They were astonishingly accurate, and to demolish an enemy sangar at 800 yards was child's play. My only sorrow was that we were not allowed many rounds for practice, owing to the short supply from the arsenal which of course had stopped manufacturing ammunition for these obsolete mountain pieces.

Two or three times a week an alarm practice was carried out to ensure that every man knew his position in the defence of the post. The signal was the blowing on a whistle, alternate long and short blasts, and any officer or NCO who sensed danger could send it.

Every post had a quarter guard of at least eight men, in some cases eleven, two of whom were NCOs. One sentry was always on duty at the gate and another above on the wall of the post to report down to the guard commander the approach of any party, friends or strangers. Besides these two sentries a third was always on duty walking round inside the walls on top.

On the sounding of the alarm the main gate was closed, leaving open the small emergency door, cut out of the main gate, to permit ingress of those left outside. All armed personnel would draw arms and ammunition and fall in on their alarm posts without delay. And so it was always possible to assess the efficiency of the commander of any post by ordering an alarm at an unspecified time and noting how quickly, efficiently and without confusion alarm stations were manned. To Sarwekai, located as it was practically in Mahsud territory only the best Militia officers were sent, and this was undoubtedly the main factor which ensured

45

our salvation a few months later. No risks could be taken in this most unfriendly locality and no one realized this more than the garrison, from the most junior sepoy to the most senior officer present.

Only a few weeks before two of our British officers had been killed in action with Mahsuds, both within a couple of miles of the post. One of these, a major and his second in command had gone out with a strong party to the top of a high hill to the south-west so as to get into direct touch with Wana by helio. All communications had been cut and it had been essential to do this to report to HQ. The party had been fiercely attacked by local Mahsuds who, in overwhelming numbers almost wiped out the entire Militia party. The other officer, a Indian Civil service man by the name of Davidson, seconded to the South Waziristan Militia, was shot dead when out with a rear party returning from some operation towards Sarwekai from the Khuzma Pass. This pass is at the head of a long low valley, through which a rocky track runs until the valley opens out somewhere close to the Nili Spinkai main track. This Khuzma track is important because it is one of the main routes used by raiding gangs, both going to and returning from the Murtaza-Tank area. A small post is situated on the track, about halfway up the valley, and therefore is in a position to intercept any gang with animals using that getaway. As loot is the main means of existence of the poorer Mahsuds, the gaining of which provides sport and excitement for the rest of them, the blocking of their escape routes was always a source of irritation for the tribes and therefore an incentive for creating trouble for the British whenever they found an opportunity.

Any movement in the close hilly country near the Mahsud border required calculated and covered advances and with-drawals. Sloppy and careless ways were sooner or later sure to bring disaster for they were watched, I noted, by unseen eyes and plans laid accordingly. Not only is it a crime in mountain warfare to move about carelessly but to repeat the same movement or operation in the same way, although carried out well, is also to invite trouble.

Life in Wana during the winter of 1917/18 continued to be peaceful and I enjoyed every minute of it. There was always some-thing interesting to absorb one's time. In the Mess we always had the most recent English illustrated weeklies, a fine library and the daily papers: *The Pioneer* and the *Civil and Military Gazette*.[12] The post arrived regularly, unless the Gomal at Khajuri happened to be in spate preventing His Majesty's mail, carried on a strong little donkey, from crossing over to the Tanai side of the river. A Mahsud *baddraga* (guard) switched along the donkey, which was changed once or twice on the trip, but the one man did the whole mileage within twenty-four hours, more than 40 miles. Being a Mahsud, of course the *baddraga* was safe.

We had a tennis court, a small swimming pool and also a sticky court. The last-named game was played with a tennis ball and a tennis racquet, but the court, about the size of a tennis court, was totally enclosed by high walls and a player was allowed to take a return off a wall, as one did at squash.

I never tired of going through our 'game' book, in which the bag of every shoot was recorded. The total year's bag often showed more than a thousand head, mostly sisi and quail. I remember a remark made on one of the pages of this shikar book: 'Also one Wazir'. I was informed by one of the chaps on that particular shoot after quail that the Commanding Officer had fired at and killed a bird when a great hullabaloo arose from behind a stack of reaped corn, more than a hundred yards away but in front of the line of guns. A Wazir emerged from the stack and showed a neat hole in one of his legs where half a dozen number eights, having for some reason or other balled, had penetrated just under the skin. The doctor was quite happy to do a small operation and the Wazir was happier still to get 50 rupees for his minor injury.

If I got bored with life I would take a few men and beat up a nullah or two within a short distance of the post, with always the chance of picking up a sisi or quail. On one such occasion I had a queer experience: I was walking in a shallow depression alongside a field of wheat with my escort and beaters extended in line just behind me, when to my astonishment a snake, thinnish and about six or perhaps seven feet long came up from behind me and flashed past and on at great speed. It disappeared up the nullah and I did not see it again. Its movement when it raced past me seemed to be hoop-like. In later years, when I thought about that incident I often wondered to myself whether I had imagined the whole affair, for how could a snake move at such speed? Later I mentioned my experience to a retired Forest Officer who was very knowledgeable on the subject of snakes, and he assured me that there are several kinds which can move rapidly when frightened. He suggested that the serpent was probably a desert cobra which is sometimes found in the North-West Frontier Province.

On occasions I would walk down to the stream, taking a light fishing rod. Below a little rocky hill, called Gibraltar, the *toi* had scooped out from under an overhanging rock a deep pool which was always sure to yield a couple of fat little snow trout or a small *mahseer*. The former are delicious when fried after being lightly covered in thin batter. Their size does not make any difference to the taste – small or large they are good to eat.

Later on in 1918, the terrible plague, Spanish Flu, arrived in South Waziristan from the countries of Persia and Afghanistan, where it had taken a dreadful toll of human lives. Hardly anyone in the South Waziristan Militia escaped its attention and in our militia alone we lost 120 men. It was so virulent and sudden that in some posts the gates had to be kept shut as there were not enough fit men to carry out guard duties with normal changes. In some cases patients discharged from hospital as fit or nearly fit, so as to make room for others, would have to be re-admitted the following day, having relapsed and collapsed with serious lung trouble. By the evening of the same day most of these relapsed cases would be dead. This appalling plague seemed to strike direct at the heart and lungs. I was fortunate to have a mild attack and was in bed only two days.

As the result of our depleted strength we had to take in a large number of recruits and their training kept us junior officers occupied for several months. Besides this I was studying to pass the higher standard Pushtu examination that was essential for my retention in militias. In that year I was successful in doing this and also in attaining the age of twenty-one.

That winter, 1918/19, was marvellous. The shooting season, from September to March, was the best Wana had had for years. There was peace in Europe, but for Waziristan this was only a lull before a storm which, of course, we did not know was coming. By April of

1919, trouble was obviously brewing on the Frontier but many of the fine troops of the Indian Army had not arrived back from overseas, and there was a shortage of good, trained battalions. The unfortunate result was that adequate support was not possible at all points. Isolated posts like Wana and Sarwekai were left to fend for themselves, or get out of the approaching upheaval as best they could. The Tochi Militia was safely supported by a brigade at Bannu and also regular troops at Miranshah. The Kurram Militia was safe and supported by a strong force at Kohat. The Mohmand Militia was closely supported by a division at Peshawar. But the South Waziristan Militia, out in the blue and in the most hostile of all areas was impossible to support. There were no regular units within range to come to our help.

I knew nothing of the approaching trouble when I was sent off to Sarwekai, to stay there until further orders. I just took my normal kit and stores and was quite unworried for a few days. However, one day the Political Agent arrived and said that he would be staying put for some time, and this unusual and long visit made me suspicious. He said no more to me and I did not question him, I just carried on with the normal routine work in the post: parades, musketry from the walls of the post, firing at white-washed stones on the hillsides at different ranges, rifle and kit inspections. On the morning of the fateful day, during the night of which we evacuated Sarwekai post and ran for our lives, the Political Agent showed me a message from the Chief Commissioner of the North-West Frontier Province,[13] under whose orders all militias functioned, ordering the evacuation from South Waziristan of the South Waziristan Militia that night. Sarwekai post had to withdraw to Murtaza direct, also the Gomal posts, while Wana and the nearby posts were to retire towards Fort Sandeman up the Zhob Valley.

With the Mahsuds actually living on our back doorstep it was clear that not the slightest hint of our intention should leak out to them until it was no longer possible to keep them in ignorance, by which time I hoped that it would be too late for them to intercept or catch up with us as we withdrew. They were not the sort of people who would waste a minute once they got to know that there was a chance to get rifles, ammunition, rations and lots of other oddments dear to their hearts, as well as a chance of slaughtering their hated enemies, us.

The Political Agent had been anxious regarding the loyalty of our men, for we had four or five different classes or tribes represented in the post. However, this did not worry me and I assured him that all would remain steadfast, that is all except for five Wazirs who, of course, could not be trusted. On and off I had spent many months in this post and had got to know all ranks well. I liked them and we always got on well together.

I had made up my mind that as far as possible, everything to be left behind would be destroyed so that all our hated enemy would find in Sarwekai would be the burnt-out shell and ashes, and in my preparations I assiduously sought to achieve this. Having ample time in which to complete arrangements I decided not to inform anyone before twelve noon and I had an early lunch for I knew that once the work started off, there would be little time for eating.

Just before twelve I called up all four of our Militia Pathan officers and in the Mess I broke the news to them. We then spent some minutes discussing the plans put forward. After making a few changes and finalizing our method we set to work to carry it out. I record here that the Militia officers I had to help me were all first-class chaps and it was entirely due to their co-operation, loyalty, advice and energy in helping to get everything going smoothly and finished on time that we all eventually got away safely and without a hitch. For the loyalty and steadfastness of my men, be all praise.

Before anyone else was told and any other steps taken, the five Wazirs were put behind bars in the cell, for none of us had any doubt that given a chance, they would try to create trouble or escape to give information to their cousins, the Mahsuds, whose nearest village, Sarkai Obo, was barely a mile away and within a few hundred yards of the track which we were to retire along. It was vital that they should not suspect what was being planned.

The alarm was then sounded, all personnel were called into the post, the gates were locked and extra sentries were posted to prevent anyone from leaving. Then, to stop any false rumours from getting round, the Indian officers told their men what we were going to do. It was impressed on all that secrecy up to the last moment, and speed with as little commotion as possible, were essential for a safe escape that night. For all ranks, food was prepared and given out for the haversack, and the midday meal eaten.

While this was being done parties of men started to make arrangements for the burning of all Quartermaster's stores, rations, kits, barracks and charpoys,[14] the Mess and officers' quarters, hospital and stores, *bunyah*'s[15] shop and so forth.

The post reserve store contained enough food for a brigade, tins and tins of kerosene oil, tins and tins of ghee, bags upon bags of atta, dhal[16] and rice, all guaranteed to make a really good blaze when the time came to set it alight. All the bags were brought out and laid out in lines. All the tins of oil and ghee were opened and some of the contents sprinkled on the bags.

All the shells, powder and other ammunition had to be exploded and, to ensure that they did not escape destruction, all the boxes and cases were opened up and kerosene oil-soaked blankets spread over the lot. In all rooms and barracks charpoys, chairs, etc. were sprinkled with oil so as to be certain that not only they, but also the rooms would not escape the fire.

The two mountain guns were rendered useless by spiking them and then smashing at the screws with a heavy hammer. Also all the sighting arrangements and the range-taking instruments were destroyed. I must admit that above all I greatly regretted having to leave behind the two guns and my bob-tailed, fat little nag.

At this time we had with us in the post five or six British other ranks who had been sent to work a small radio station in case, as had happened before communications were disrupted at the critical moment. To send messages they had a little Douglas twin-opposed engine worked by petrol. This was on a metal frame and attached to a dynamo which provided the necessary current.

All was ready before darkness set in and parties and commanders had been told. The Political Agent, the British officer reservists and the main body fell in, set to go. They had their own advance guard and rear party, and consisted of everyone except my own small rear party of one Militia officer and twenty soldiers.

The gates were opened, the main party went out into the dark night as silently as possible. Then we shut the gates again and waited. I hoped and prayed that no Mahsud would come to know of the departure of the first party or, if one did that he would think that it was only some night operation that was being done.

Our group now had an hour to wait before setting everything alight. This hour, I felt, was as much as we could allow before the rest of us followed. We knew that within an hour of the post going up in smoke and flames the Mahsuds from the nearby villages would be on their way up to investigate. That meant that the main party would have at least two hours' start of any following Mahsuds and that my group would have one hour's start. This would be enough.

That one hour seemed an age. We spent the time making torches for the men who were to set fire to the different rooms and places. Then, when there were a few minutes to go we shooed the animals out to safety. When the hour was up we sent the firing party round the post. They had to do their jobs as rapidly as possible, starting from the Officers' Mess and coming down towards the gate. The kerosene oil-soaked blankets covering the shells, powder and ammunition were set alight last of all by the Indian officer and myself. The gates had been opened, the five Wazirs had disappeared into the night, and the rest of us ran out and away at a steady jog in a compact body.

The track we ran down silently and the track the Mahsuds would use in coming to the post as soon as they saw it ablaze, was the same one. We had to get down the ridge and along that track about three-quarters of a mile before branching off safely to the right along the Khuzma road. Luckily we had almost completed that three-quarters of a mile before the flames had started to shoot, in huge long tongues into the sky, outlining the walls of the fort in a vivid glare. As we turned off to the safe track, illuminating shells, which I had never seen fired, soared, one after the other, into the air to light up the long Sarwekai ridge. And the roar of exploding shells and boxes of powder and ammunition shattered the otherwise stillness of the night, and I knew that the tribes, from different directions, would now be converging on the post. However, they would not start to follow after us until they were quite satisfied there was nothing to be salvaged from Sarwekai post, by which time we would be at least three miles on our way and no following gang would be able to catch up with us. My anxiety left me and I was able to take a few glances over my right shoulder to look back and enjoy a wonderful fireworks display, paid for by the British Raj because of its neglect in supporting a vulnerable little garrison.

The going was good as far as Khuzma Marai and we made fast progress. But when we started on the descent, and mile after mile of it because the steep track was hardly a track in many places and barely discernible in the dark, we had to slow down. It was difficult to place a foot on a spot where there wasn't a wobbly stone. After three or four hours of going we came to the small post of Khuzma in the valley, but found that it was deserted, for the main body had collected the garrison as they went past.

In Waziristan the summer starts early and as we proceeded lower the heat in the closed valley became oppressive and we soon had to halt for a minute or two for a drink from our water bottles. My orderly carried mine, I carried nothing, and I don't think I could have made it had I been burdened with a lot of stuff. By now, for more than twelve hours I had been at full blast without rest and I expect that, and the anxiety of the whole affair, were beginning to make themselves felt, but to get on, get on we had to. It was our only hope. For a few more hours we half-ran, half-walked on towards safety. A new day began to dawn on us as we arrived at a place where our Khuzma track showed a branching path to the left. This track led to the small posts of Tormandu and Mudhussan, which I have mentioned earlier in my story. We took this way, although it is longer by a couple of miles than the main Wana-Spinkai-Murtaza road, because we wanted to satisfy our-selves that our men in those two posts were safely out of those horrible death traps.

Dawn was now breaking. As the sun touched the tops of the higher mountains our party came to the last valley and the last ridge which we had to pass. Both Tormandu and Mudhasan posts were empty, having been called in by someone that night and so we were not delayed further and soon emerged on to the plain, or *raghza*, and left Waziristan behind our backs. My small party was now safe. We slowed down as there was no further danger and walked at a gentle pace to Murtaza. An hour later we entered the gates of that post to find to our relief that our friends from the Gomal posts as well as our own Sarwekai people had all arrived safely. They had been anxiously looking out for us to appear from the Spinkai gap but, of course we had taken the other route. It transpired that by going the other way, we had most probably avoided a nasty encounter with following tribesmen in pursuit of Percy Clery and the Gomal posts' garrisons because, half an hour after we got in, the crests of the Spinkai ridge which overlooked the plains of India were crowded with tribesmen. There were hundreds, if not thousands of them and not long afterwards they swept down onto the plain, but gave Murtaza a wide berth.

The Political Agent and the five British officer reservists had departed for Tank in transport, which had been arranged for them, and I never saw them again. But I was told that they were all right, although suffering from painful swollen ankles. That I could quite understand, as mine were not feeling too good after that long midnight descent down the rocky Khuzma pass.

That night, in my prayers, I thanked Almighty God for safely delivering my companions and me. I remembered David's beautiful 23rd Psalm that I had learnt, as a child, at my mother's knee.

And what did the tribesmen think of this unexpected, overnight retreat of the forces of the British from their territory? I never asked a Mahsud or Wazir what they had thought about it, but from the consequent and unrestricted invasions by huge bands of marauding Wazirs and Mahsuds, who started their depredations within an hour or two of our getting into Murtaza, it was obvious to all and sundry that the inhabitants of Waziristan were convinced that the British were on the run and that it was now their innings, and that they could occupy some of our country, or at any rate help themselves to whatever they wanted in the way of loot of every kind.

The Frontier Constabulary under the redoubtable 'Handy' were kept busy day and night, protecting this or that village or area threatened by reported *lashkars*. It was mainly the responsibility of this corps to ensure the safety of villages in Indian borderlands and, because of their special training in this type of work, they and the armed police were best suited for it. However, because of the alarming increase of concerted attacks and minor raids in every direction, it became impossible for them to cope with all of our calls for help, and two squadrons of Indian cavalry were called in to help.

On the morning after our arrival at Murtaza one of these squadrons from a fine unit arrived at the Murtaza area and when out towards the Mudhassan *narai*,[17] on the *raghza*, came across a large party of Mahsuds on their way down to the Tank area. The tribesmen, not relishing an encounter with a regular horse-mounted unit on the level, began to withdraw to their hills and this was exactly what the *Rissala*[18] looked for – in their charge they slew most of the raiders. But when the squadron returned after their short but glorious battle, there was great sorrow in that sub-unit for their Rissaldar, a very fine Indian officer, and three or four other ranks had been killed in the fight. Well, the Mahsuds had had their first lesson and now knew that for them all was not going to be plain sailing.

The Frontier Constabulary held many small posts along the border with tribal territory, three of which were within reasonable distance of Murtaza, where by now our South Waziristan Militia strength there had risen to over 400. These three posts began to feel the pinch of shortage of food and called for help. *Lashkars* had cut off all supplies from reaching them and one convoy, escorted by some cavalry from an inexperienced Indian state, had met with disaster within five miles of our post. Everything in the convoy, including the camels, had fallen into the tribesmen's hands, a really fine haul for them.

There were now only two of us officers in Murtaza with our South Waziristan Militia: Percy Clery, who had brought in the garrisons of the Gomal posts, and myself. As I happened to be the senior the onus of command fell on me for the time being. When instructions arrived from our Indian officers' Frontier Constabulary to take orders from the local Civil people, it meant that we would be expected to carry out the normal duties of the Frontier Constabulary, who were clearly being overworked.

Our first job was to relieve a post held by the Frontier Constabulary to the south of the post and within 10 miles. Having heard about the disaster that had overtaken the last relieving convoy, I took no risks and escorted the one we were taking with 300 of our Militia. As we went along I posted picquets between our route and the hills, where the enemy were lurking. These strongpoints were left out to cover us in when we withdrew later on in the day. The convoy of camels had assembled and loaded up at Murtaza so we had been able to make an early start with the result that, after relieving the posts (the garrisons of which were overjoyed to see us come with lots of atta, rice, ghee, oil and a few boxes of ammunition) we were able to make our way back before nightfall. We next relieved Girni, a strong little fort below an enormous hill, Girni Sar. This was about five miles to the north of us, along the *raghza* where the cavalry had made their charge against the Mahsuds, and was an easy operation without any danger of interference, as the terrain was easy and my escorting Militia in good strength.

After these two small operations we were called out on several occasions to march a few miles in different directions to succour villages threatened by large gangs. We usually moved out just before dark, being shown the way by a villager or Frontier Constabulary man. Our reason for leaving at this hour was that we hoped the raiding parties, not seeing our men arrive, would attack and give us or the Frontier Constabulary, who sometimes combined with us, a chance to inflict casualties. However, we were left unmolested and no village which we were sent to help was attacked. On one occasion I found myself in a large scattered village which, a report said, was definitely going to be attacked that night. I met Handy there, for he had also been told about the impending assault. Both of us got down to making careful and strong dispositions with our men, who were in good strength, but we waited in vain throughout the night and departed in the morning, disappointed, to our respective headquarters.

It was about this time, after we had been moved from Murtaza to Tank, that details got to us about the dreadful tragedy that had overtaken the Wana party. Due to the long distance they had to withdraw from Wana, the Commanding Officer had decided to halt for one night at a post on the route. This delay resulted in the column's disaster for it enabled Wazirs and Mahsuds, who were following close on their heels, to occupy positions overlooking the Zhob route which they had to take. On the following morning our party had to fight to get past these enemy positions and in this battle we suffered heavy casualties. Four officers were killed, two wounded and two got away unhurt. Of the four who died, one was the garrison engineer. The four officers who managed to get away were helped by the Zhob Militia who came down to render what assistance they could. Eventually our four officers, one of whom was our Militia doctor, arrived at Fort Sandeman and later were taken to Quetta, where my father visited the two wounded officers in hospital and so got all the news about the evacuation.

Many of our Militiamen had been killed but a few managed to escape through the hills, moving at night, and rejoined us. One person who arrived back, and whom Percy and I were very glad to see again, was our dear old white-bearded mess cook. He knew of only one good way down to India and that was by the Gomal route and not by Fort Sandeman. So he had trudged along slowly down the main track by himself, and the Mahsuds had let him go free, for he was aged. Within a day or two he was back in the kitchen cooking our meals and, after having to eat our men's food for many days, Percy and I at last had what we liked.

We heard that our commanding officer, Major Russell, who had been badly wounded in the battle, had been put in for the Victoria Cross for his magnificent leadership and courage, but we were all disappointed when he was awarded the Distinguished Service Order instead. Another of our young officers of the Wana garrison, Barker, was awarded the Military Cross for his conspicuous courage in the withdrawal. He was the only officer of that Wana party who returned to serve with our Militia. Two of the Militia's British officers who lost their lives in the last action had joined us only a week or two before the evacuation and therefore had had little experience in Frontier warfare. The impossible had been expected from the isolated garrison of Wana and it was no fault of any officer there that disaster had struck.

That summer in Tank was unbelievably hot. The day temperatures soared to a dreadful 125° F. To make matters worse for our men, the Mohammedan fast, Raza, happened to come round at that time. According to their religion and its laws all good Mohammedans are expected to refrain from food and water from early morning to sundown. Although there are provisions in the law excusing the adhering to these rules under certain conditions, most of the men preferred to keep the Raza and I hate to think what agonies these poor chaps went through during that blazing summer. A war was in progress and we had to move about during the heat of the day on some occasions although, of course, we tried to limit this as much as possible.

The protection of the threatened villages and running of trains had to be done. Roving bands of infiltrators spread terror throughout the border areas of the North-West Frontier Province and not only where we were. The lands round the large cantonments of Bannu, Kohat and even Peshawar were not without daily skirmishes, murders and kidnappings. Nowhere was life and property immune from attack by raiding gangs, and every success achieved by one marauding party encouraged other, otherwise peaceful people, to join in the scramble for loot. In the large military station of Kohat the murder of one member of a British family, and the kidnapping of the daughter, fairly shook the authorities, not only in India but also in Britain. The story of the outstanding courage of a British missionary lady, who went into tribal territory and persuaded the Afridi clan holding the girl to release her, appeared in all the papers.

The Bannu-Kalabagh and Tank-Kalabagh trains and the intermediate stations on those lines were not left unmolested, and strong guards had to accompany them. In fact it looked as though there were just not sufficient soldiers, Frontier Constabulary and armed police to cope with the troubles. The Frontier was ablaze and savage warfare, with gloves off, continued for some time. Those of us officers who, because of serving on the Frontier, had missed the battles that had been fought at Flanders, Gaza and Kut, were now having our turn. Percy and I had one most acceptable compensation for we were lent a nice bungalow in Tank. The Political Resident of Waziristan, who had been kind enough to let us use this house, was a very keen gardener and had been in the Militias before transferring to Political. In 1916, I had met him in Miranshah when he was in the Tochi Militia and I remember well the first-class garden he ran for that Militia. It was so filled with vegetables that he was even able to supply our battalion Mess with our requirements. His bungalow in Tank had a large and beautifully kept lawn in front and this helped to keep the temperature down, especially once the sun had departed in its lurid descent. It was here that we sat and chatted after dinner on the day we were not out in the countryside, and it was to this lovely grass area that our servants brought out our beds, the coolest spot in Tank, when it was time to sleep.

A few days after being ordered in from Murtaza for garrisoning Tank, and being closer to the scene of operations, a couple of British officers from other militias arrived to reinforce us and to give Percy and myself a chance to rest. One was a major, who now took over command until our permanent commanding officer, who had been away on home leave, returned.

A few weeks later Percy and I were allowed to go on a few days' short leave which we were badly in need of. By the time we rejoined, the South Waziristan Militia had moved to Dera Ismael Khan[19] where, under canvas, we were given a chance to reorganize. Thank heaven our permanent commanding officer was back with us. A pre-war officer and a senior major, he was exactly what we needed to pull together. For months we had been harried about with never a chance to settle down, do a parade ground exercise or carry out rifle practice. Teddy Davis was senior enough to persuade the authorities concerned to allow us the time necessary to reform, smarten up and re-equip. Within a few weeks everything had been attended to and the South Waziristan Militia soon took on the appearance of a well-disciplined unit, such as we had been before when in Waziristan, before the evacuation.

Dera Ismael Khan was a good location to be in as head-quarters of a district. There were many Europeans in residence and it boasted of a club where a member could play bridge, tennis, squash or enjoy a swim in a large-sized swimming pool. At nights the air was cool and the River Indus flows close by and, in any case, we were stationed there in the autumn and early winter.

Bombing planes had made their first appearance on the Frontier about that time, and a squadron was stationed at a place called Manwali, not far down the line from Dera Ismael Khan. I had seen an aeroplane for the first time when on my short leave in Quetta and was quite keen to bag a flight if ever given the chance. This opportunity arrived sooner than I expected. The political pundits had heard that some Afghan tribes had arrived in Wana to garrison the political Sarai, which lay about half a mile to the south of Wana. The Army, on hearing this interesting bit of news wanted the Sarai bombed and our commanding officer asked me if I would volunteer to fly in a bomber to show the pilot the correct target. Naturally I was thrilled at the thought and before long I was in Manwali being introduced to the Squadron Commander, an officer not much older than myself but with the left side of his tunic one mass of decorations. I was quite awed at the sight and wondered how on earth one man could collect such a breast-full of *bahaduries*.[20] He turned out to be a jolly good fellow and put me at ease in a minute. In his office there hung an enormous map and it was quite easy for me to find Wana.

It was decided that our aircraft, with a full load of bombs, would take off just after dawn on the morrow. The pilot, the officer who controlled the bomb-releasing devices and myself climbed into our tandem seats in the dark hour before dawn. The two engines were started up and allowed to run for a few minutes to warm up. Then we roared up the *maidan*,[21] gathering speed until we must have been doing 60 to 80 miles per hour. After a few hundred yards I noticed that we were still skimming along the ground and were not in the air. I began to worry, for not very far ahead, looming up in the distance, was a dark line which, as we got nearer proved to be the end of the *maidan* marked by high trees. I was getting scared and I expect the pilot was too, for he switched down both engines suddenly. We came to a standstill within 10 or 15 yards of the line of trees. The engines had been left ticking over and we turned and taxied back to the starting line. I remained aboard while the others discussed matters and some airmen made an adjustment or two. From the odd word I heard, I gathered that we were slightly overloaded with petrol and bombs and that perhaps some tank had been badly filled. Anyway, after fifteen minutes' delay, by which time dawn had broken, we were screaming along the runway again, this time becoming airborne quickly and, gaining height, were soon up to almost 2,000 feet, at which height we seemed to remain as we headed towards our objective.

It is now fifty years since that exciting and for me frightening episode. And when I recall our escape in the De Havilland 10 loaded with bombs and petrol, from bumping into the line of trees which bordered the airfield, a cold feeling runs down my spine. We had surely narrowly escaped a rapid cremation.

As we flew on I was very interested in trying to recognize the places I had been to, but we were passing over country about 30 miles to the south of Tank and I only began to see places I knew when we got to the vicinity of Tanai and Karabkot. We arrived dead on to the Wana plain so I was immediately able to point out the Civil Sarai. After circling a couple of times the De Havilland 10 went down, diving towards the target at tremendous speed with the many wires, which seemed to hold the wings, vibrating in song. Bombs were released and I was able to watch them going down till they exploded. We climbed up again to make another swoop at the target and, circling once more, dived and let go the remainder of the explosives. I was disappointed, for not one bomb hit the Sarai, the nearest having fallen about 10 yards to the north. By this time we hadn't any spare petrol for sightseeing, so headed for home. We landed safely at the aerodrome and I got down. We found that the wings of the aircraft were perforated in several places by bullet holes, so we had been under quite accurate fire and I had known nothing about it at the time.

Were I invited today to go for a flip in a De Havilland 10, my answer would not be in the affirmative. When I had stuck my head over the edge of my cockpit to watch the bombs drop, it very nearly followed them. And those wires! Afterwards, I wondered what would have happened had bullets snipped one or two. Two months later I watched a single-engine plane being shot down by Mahsud rifle fire – I shall be writing about that incident later on in my story. But when I look back through the years and remember these incidents and the hundreds of times one was sniped at during the operations in Waziristan, I am convinced that being fired at from long range when on the ground was preferable to being fired at when in the air. As my old friend our head clerk replied when asked whether he would prefer to be involved in a train accident or an air accident, 'In a train accident, there you are. But in an air accident, where you are?'

While we were in Dera Ismael Khan in the early winter of 1919/20, a strong force was assembling at Manzai, Khirgi and Jandola. The first named was west of Tank and just cis-border. Khirgi camp and Jandola post and camp were on the Taki Zam stream and across the border. The three streams, the Gomal, the Taki

61

Zam and the Tochi, all flowed from west to east: the Gomal from south Waziristan; 10 miles north the Taki Zam from central Waziristan; and 20 or 30 miles further north the Tochi flowed through north Waziristan. Jandola post was about five miles inside the Waziristan hills and was to be the kicking-off place for the assembling force, which was called the Waziristan Field Force. It was clear that the British had decided something had to be done to restore the 'loss of face' which Government had suffered and were still suffering. One thing was clear: the force was collecting to move into the heart of Mahsud territory, for it was this tribe that was responsible for most of the depredations carried out in the past few months.

One day, at the end of January 1920, the Commanding Officer sent for me to say that he had been asked by the Army to attach 100 Scouts to the Waziristan Field Force for service with the forward brigades. He asked me if I would like to go along with them and, if so, I could select my men. This was a wonderful offer and I agreed at once. My friend Percy Clery, who had shared with me the thrills and dangers of the evacuation, and also many other small operations we had been on during the hot months of 1919, volunteered to accompany me.

I insisted that everyone had to be a volunteer and that the four Militia Indian officers we had asked gave in the names of the men and non-commissioned officers from this small but magnificent body of Pathan fighters. The South Waziristan Militia, when reformed a few years later, took the name South Waziristan Scouts.

Our Scouts were given exactly the same stores, clothing and equipment as were issued to the Regular troops. High up in the Mahsud hills the weather was going to be bitterly cold so everyone had gloves, balaclavas, mufflers and extra blankets. Two pairs of thick army socks and a pair of heavy ammunition boots were offered for each soldier. The former were gladly accepted but the latter politely refused. No Militia soldier is ever seen wearing boots when on operations, for he knows that to be able to fight on level terms with his enemies he must be as swift moving as they are. Anyone with a pair of army boots on his feet is seriously handicapped right from the beginning when fighting in the hills against tribesmen.

We were issued with the new charger-loading rifles, our old but faithful long-barrelled Lee Enfield single loaders were taken away and we never saw them again. Of course the men were delighted with their new weapons and it did not require any encouragement on the part of the officers to get them to practise rapid loading and unloading.

Dera Ismael Khan is about 40 miles from Tank, which is another 15 or so miles from Manzai, so we had a three-day march to do before we joined the Waziristan Field Force there. During this march we were given the job of escorting a British mobile howitzer battery of 4.5 guns, also on their way to join the force.

The day came when with the Commanding Officer's blessing and hundreds of 'Pah makh a de kha' and 'Khudai de mal sha' ('May God be with you' and 'May you be God's special care') we marched out of our camp to rendezvous with the battery a mile or so up the road. The British gunners, officers and men palled up with us and our chaps in no time and that night, when in camp, our lads gave a *khattak*[22] dance round a bonfire. The gunners had been issued with rifle chains and I explained to the Commanding Officer about using them from then onwards owing to the prevalence in this part of the land of rifle thieves who, in addition to rifles, did not disdain a revolver if it could fall into their hands as the result of an easy theft. The first night out required special precautions against marauders and we surrounded our camp with sentry groups. Tank, we now found, was a wired-in camp so there was no danger from outside, except the chance of thieving. On the third day we marched to Manzai. Here our escorting job ended and we halted for a few days.

The first night we spent in Manzai is, for me, unforgettable. The post is built on a long flat-topped ridge and overlooked, at a few hundred yards, by another low ridge on which at one place stands a small blockhouse that does not command the whole expanse of its spur. The very extensive camp has no perimeter wall but is protected by a number of sangared picquets, about 80 yards apart, and situated on the double wire defences. That night some local snipers, who could not have been Mahsuds (for they were waiting at Jansola to defend their land) opened up with rifle fire on the camp, the battalion holding the camp picquets became jumpy and within seconds were firing off their Very light pistols, whose illuminating charges hissed into the air all round the camp. The firers, not taking into account whether they fired red, green or white cartridges kept the fireworks display going until officers went round the picquets and stopped the fun. Some of the men in the picquets even fired into the night with rifles and Lewis guns. Heaven alone knows what they were hoping to hit.

The next day the Force Commander at Khirgi wanted to know if Manzai had repulsed a heavy Mahsud night attack. They had seen and heard what had gone on, for Khirgi post is only about three miles away and stands higher and in full view.

At Manzai we were kept busy going out daily, either towards Tank or up towards Khirgi, on road protection duty. However, only once were we fired on when out on this work and that incident was more amusing than serious.

Normally, when out between Manzai and Khirgi, the camel convoys took the direct route, a very rough track which in some places passed through broken ground covered in low bushes. But one day we were asked to escort the returning convoy from Khirgi along a steep gorge that runs just north of the long Manzai-Khirgi ridge. We were told that this way was shorter than the other and also safer from attack by gangs of tribesmen, who on one or two occasions, hiding close to the track in the bushes and rocks, had made lightning assaults on the convoy, making off with camels loaded with supplies, after knifing the unfortunate unarmed camel man. When it is understood that the replenishing of supplies for a couple of brigades and hundreds of animals required the carrying capacity of hundreds of camels, and that a huge convoy, even proceeding along in two or three lines could well spread back along the route for half a mile or even more, then it can be realized that there are likely to occur large gaps between the groups of escorting soldiers. The thieves, looking out for such gaps while lying doggo, take their opportunity while accepting the risks. Once a string of animals is detached, a couple of men switch them along unmercifully at a fast gallop until they reach the cover of the hills. To give chase would be just a waste of time, for not only can they move as fast as the pursuer but they have had the start of them and, moreover, are quite likely to have some men with rifles covering the getaway. The best safeguard is to have picqueting troops out as well as supplying an escort to move along with the convoy. Apparently the powers that be had considered picqueting an almost flat portion of the track unnecessary. Thank heaven the South Waziristan Scouts never lost a camel from any convoy they escorted.

[Editor's note: Cumming's first experience in battle with the tribesmen left him shaken by the terrible sight of 'stretcher after stretcher' being carried from the battlefront. The British losses in these engagements with the Pathans were of a magnitude not seen since the days of the 1857 Sepoy Mutiny. It became commonplace for British Indian and Regular Army troops to sustain hundreds of casualties in these clashes in Waziristan. In other parts of India, when native armies suffered defeat at the hands of British artillery and cavalry, they would eventually be absorbed into the Empire and became more or less peaceful subjects of the British Raj. Not so the Pathans. The Pathans call their homeland Yaghistan, the 'Land of the Untamed'. Any British soldiers who served on the North-West Frontier would acknowledge that the name is fully justified. No doubt the conquerors of past centuries, whose armies clashed with these hill tribes, would also endorse this view. Over the centuries, the tribesmen of this harsh and arid land have been moulded into what has often been called the world's toughest fighting men. The Pathans' ability to stalk an enemy with the stealth and cunning of a panther is legendary. Their power of moving concealed is astounding, not only in darting from cover to cover, but in slipping from light to shadow, and background to background. When a tribal army, known as a *lashkar*, was defeated, the elders and maliks would be called to a *jirga* to negotiate their fate. The *jirga*, or council, forms the backbone of Pathan democracy. The earliest records of formal *jirgas* stretch back many centuries and there is documentary evidence of these meetings having been held in Kandahar as early as 72 BC. The *jirga* leaders would usually be called upon to surrender their weapons and pay a fine, and they would give an undertaking to refrain from raiding the so-called 'settled areas' under direct British administration. The problem, as Cumming would painfully learn, was that they rarely complied for long with these demands, particularly the recalcitrant Mahsuds of South Waziristan, who did not consider themselves obliged to abide by rulings of their village elders.]

DISCOVER MORE ABOUT MILITARY HISTORY

Pen & Sword Books have over 1500 titles in print covering all aspects of military history on land, sea and air. If you would like to receive more information and special offers on your preferred interests from time to time along with our standard catalogue, please complete your areas of interest below and return this card (no stamp required in the UK). Alternatively, register online at www.pen-and-sword.co.uk. Thank you.

PLEASE NOTE: We do not sell data information to any third party companies

Mr/Mrs/Ms/Other............Name............

Address............

............Postcode............

Email address............

If you wish to receive our email newsletter, please tick here ☐

PLEASE SELECT YOUR AREAS OF INTEREST

Ancient History ☐	Medieval History ☐	English Civil War ☐
Napoleonic ☐	Pre World War One ☐	World War One ☐
World War Two ☐	Post World War Two ☐	Falklands ☐
Aviation ☐	Maritime ☐	Battlefield Guides ☐
Regimental History ☐	Military Reference ☐	Military Biography ☐

Website: www.pen-and-sword.co.uk • Email: enquiries@pen-and-sword.co.uk
Telephone: 01226 734555 • Fax: 01226 734438

Pen & Sword Books
FREEPOST SF5
47 Church Street
BARNSLEY
South Yorkshire
S70 2BR

2

If posting
from outside
of the UK
please affix
stamp here

Chapter 3

Slugging it out at Ahnai

January 1920

Harking back to an incident I had begun to tell about, we were protecting as an escort a convoy of hundreds of camels along the north track through a steep-sided gorge. This unhealthy track had steep precipitous sides that gave little or no opportunity of getting up on the right or left until approaching Manzai. I was walking along with one of the groups of my men at the rear end of the convoy, when a single sniper opened fire on us from some little distance back. He must have been hidden in some small hole in the cliff edge and screened by a bush, for it was impossible to locate him. We had to grin and bear the nasty attention he was giving us. He was using some sort of muzzle-loading ancient piece, for the interval between his shots was about the length of time it would take to reload a muzzle-loader.[1] The lumps of iron or lead which came in our direction, quite inaccurately, buzzed with the sound of a flying dung beetle and, missing us and the animals, struck the side of the cliff with resounding smacks. But we were soon round a bend and safe from further slugs.

At last we were ordered to join the Force at Jandola and marched along, past Khirgi and up the Taki Zam valley, which in some places narrows to almost a gorge. We escorted our own camel convoy that carried the men's bedding, each of which was rolled and tied up separately, tents for the men, Indian officers, British officers and followers, cooking arrangements for all personnel, picks and shovels, canvas tanks and water carriers (*pakhals*) and our reserve ammunition. When our small convoy arrived at Jandola camp a battle was in progress about a mile away across the Taki

67

Zam to the north. We had been allotted a camping space inside the camp and not on the perimeter, so had no wall to build. While our men put our camp up Percy and I and our senior Militia officer, Subedar[2] Major Makam Khan, OBI, IOM, IDSM, a local Mahsud who came from Jandola itself, which is a Bittani village, watched the withdrawal action which our troops were fighting to get back to camp after a recce towards Palosina, the Force's first objective. The rearguard was being followed up by parties of Mahsuds who used every small depression and cover to get to close quarters and inflict casualties. We could see for ourselves that the enemy were succeeding in their tactics for very soon the withdrawal was brought to a standstill to enable the casualties to be taken back. In this more casualties were suffered and, to extricate the troops involved, a small counter-attack was made – even this got into trouble in the diminishing light. The pressing enemy were not slow to take full advantage of the opportunities the delay caused. Awed by what was taking place within rifle shot of the camp, we gazed in horror. Behind us in the camp were about eight battalions of troops concentrated for the advance into Mahsudland, but not one of these was sent out to succour the hard-pressed soldiers trying to make camp and at the same time bring in their dead and wounded.

This was the first time in my service that I had witnessed battle and I must admit that I was shaken as stretcher after stretcher was carried past, where we stood, in an endless stream. On some were dead and on others grievously wounded, groaning men and one or two British officers. Eventually the tired troops staggered back into camp under cover of dusk. Our casualties in that first battle could not have been less than sixty, many of whom were left out, the wounded to be slaughtered by the Mahsuds who knew no mercy, and all to be stripped naked and mutilated. This was apparent to all on the following morn when the battlefield was searched and the atrocities brought to light. Some bodies were minus their heads, others lacking hands and feet, many slashed open. It was apparent, in this war, no quarter would be expected or given, sickening to contemplate.

Watching that battle, I learnt more about Mahsud tactics and what would be necessary to counteract them, than I could have by listening to a hundred lectures on mountain warfare. It was just as well for me that I had witnessed such a bloody encounter at the beginning of that war. I still remember these lessons.

Our commanders also had a lesson to learn. For if that sanguinary encounter wasn't a clear indication of what lay ahead, I can't think what else it could have been. While that first battle was being lost hundreds, nay thousands of tribesmen could be seen with the naked eye as they crowded along the crest of a long high ridge running north and south within a mile or two of the camp, all within easy range of our two batteries of mountain guns, the 4.5 Hero Bland, which were in action and just waiting for the order 'Fire!' that was never given to them. A heaven-sent opportunity, and what a lost opportunity. That day's undoubted defeat would have been turned into a glorious victory, for those tribesmen on those heights would not have been able to save themselves from the devastating salvos of sixteen guns, moreover for the loss of not one extra man on our side. What a boost it would have given to our men and what a setback for the Wazirs as a whole. Also it should be remembered that every casualty inflicted on the enemy would have meant at least three of their numbers out of action for some days. I heard it said that our commanders held the view, 'Were we to open on them and frighten them, they would not attack or stand and fight another day.' What a dreadful miscalculation. Never again was such a wonderful chance presented to us free, gratis and for nothing. I am an infantryman and my heart burned within me. But those gunners, it was just as well that the Force Commander, although present did not hear some of their remarks.

Eventually severe losses were inflicted on the enemy, but not without very severe losses on our side. In the battles that were fought in the following six or seven days, I doubt whether we sustained less than 1,400 casualties, including twenty British officers, these by the one leading brigade reinforced by one or two Gurkha battalions brought up to replace badly mauled troops. These battalions, which suffered severely because of inexperience in Frontier fighting, could not be blamed. Their men did not lack guts, but wars against savage tribesmen in their own hilly country must be fought out by units that have been trained in the requirements of that specialized type of fighting.

When the leading battalion, to which we were attached, moved on towards Palosina, our first camp, our Scouts were detailed to guard the north-eastern flank where the battle had started the previous day. However, except for some sniping we had no casualties or trouble, for the Mahsud and Wazir *lashkars* were combining to withstand the occupation of the camp and important picquets were needed for the protection of Palosina and the forward advance.

As soon as the brigade transport and camel train passed through on the way to the camp, we were withdrawn and on arriving were put on to building a portion of the perimeter wall. A tremendous battle was in progress. The tribesmen had without doubt made plans and preparations for it, and were fighting with their traditional ferocity and in the defence of their country.

Palosina camp was established and occupied on a small *raghza* which sloped from the west, where it ended in a high rocky ridge to the east for two or three hundred yards. Also sloping down towards the east from the west on either side of Palosina were two features, which at their extremities were high and formidable. Both of these had to be occupied while strong permanent picquets were being built on their crests. These two features had been taken by our attacking battalions and the picquets were being constructed for occupation that night to protect the camp itself, when the enemy launched fierce counter-attacks on both positions with overwhelming numbers and, after some hand-to-hand fighting, drove our troops back. By the time these attacks were made our Scouts had arrived in camp and so we witnessed the fierce action.

The enemy followed the retreating troops down the long slopes of both hills, leaping on to the backs of wounded stragglers, knifing them and snatching their rifles from their hands. A Sikh Pioneer battalion was on the right and fought with magnificent courage to defend the picquet which they had been in the process of constructing. From the camp we could see them using their clubbed rifles, not having time to reload them. All those brave men in the picquet were killed and the tribesmen swarmed into the sangar position, which was half-finished. This was the opportunity the

British howitzer battery commander had been waiting for and this time he was not kept from opening fire with rapid salvos of high explosives on the ridge. With astounding accuracy every shell landed on the picquet position and the crest, and the bodies of Mahsuds could be seen being flung into the air by the explosions. Then, when the tribesmen ran to escape the dreadful carnage-causing shells, the guns fired shrapnel that pursued them down the reverse slope of the hill. Some of my men, although not having been involved in any of the fighting, went on to the hill to help back or carry back wounded. One of them was wounded while doing this stretcher-bearer work but refused to be admitted to the field hospital for evacuation.

A Frontier Force rifles battalion on the left flank was also in trouble, with swarms of enemy harassing them. With complete disregard of danger some of them ran after our soldiers, who were getting back to a covering position, and were shot 200 yards from the camp. The Taki Zam stream ran by immediately south of the campsite, and the south bank of this was precipitous. I saw one such tribesman, who was himself killed later, push one of our badly wounded men over the cliff within a 150 yards of our perimeter. This shows the extent to which a Mahsud is prepared to risk his life to get a rifle.

We were told by the Political people that the Wazirs (including Mahsuds) suffered 400 casualties that day. I feel that figure was an underestimate. Our own casualties certainly did not total any less. All the units in the actual fighting had suffered heavily. Battle honours could, perhaps, be said to be even. Our troops had established a camp at Palosina but we had been unable, that day, to hold two hills and the picquets that had to be built on them. Due to the fighting which continued until dusk, the protective arrangements of the camp itself had only been sketchily carried out, and that night it was feared that there might be a concerted rush made on the camp by a *lashkar*. However, this failed to materialize, most probably because the enemy were fully occupied in collecting their own wounded and dead to send them back to their villages, and also to reorganize for the morrow's battle.

The following day the engagement for the same two heights was fought again. Both hilltops were occupied and the rebuilding of the two picquets, which had been badly damaged by our artillery fire, was hurried on with. The picquet on the right flank, where the Muzbi Sikh battalion of Pioneers had put up such a courageous fight the day before was named Pioneer Picquet in their honour. This picquet was built to accommodate a substantial garrison of about a hundred, including a British officer. With strong double rows of barbed-wire fencing it was made impregnable to attack by the Mahsuds.

The second, left-flank picquet, Mandana, much to our disgrace was not only badly constructed, but also badly sited in that it was overlooked slightly by the crest of the same ridge at about a hundred yards range, and no buffer wall was built across the inside of the sangar. Also, the wiring was badly done and left unfinished, withdrawal from the ridge commencing before the picquet was properly and safely occupied by the troops detailed to garrison it. Whether this withdrawal was prematurely forced upon our left flank troops by attacking tribesmen, who were there on that flank in their thousands, or whether there was a mistake in the timing of the move, I was unable to find out. But as usually follows, the *lashkars*, which had been awaiting this kind of opportunity, made their massive attack at that time.

Our right flank held firm, for Pioneer Picquet had been well built, was not overlooked and had been safely occupied well in time by our troops. Although the enemy were in the vicinity in great strength, they were unable to do much damage in the withdrawal on that side, as their own retirement would have been endangered by the strongly held Pioneer Picquet.

The fight, which now began to rage on the left flank, the Mandana Kach ridge and the long slope, was as fierce in its intensity as that which had occurred the day before. Hand-to-hand fighting took place along the ridge between the tribesmen and those men of the battalion who were waiting their turn to move back. With great courage the Indian soldiers of the Frontier Force Rifles battalion, Sikhs, Punjabi Mohds, Dogras and Pathans fought back the concerted attacks of the Mahsuds and Wazirs. Eventually they were forced back, but not until they had extracted a heavy toll from the attacking tribesmen, who now commanded the whole Mandana ridge and were able to bring fire to bear on the picquet. The defenders had hardly taken up their positions when the swarms of attackers, quickly appreciating the weakness of the sangared picquet, poured volley after volley into the semi-protected men, most of whom were killed or wounded. A party of Mahsuds now rushed down the slope at incredible speed and, leaping over the imperfectly finished wire and climbing over the wall, entered the sangar and soon knifed and slew any survivors. I was witness to this later portion of the battle which took place in the afternoon. Up to then I had been out with our Scouts protecting the road for the up convoy, which later returned on the way back to Jandola with their *khajawa* stretchers,[3] one on either side of each camel, carrying our wounded of the previous day's fight.

Our mountain battery of six guns and the howitzer battery of four again caused great havoc in the enemy ranks, for the targets they offered were perfect in their simplicity, all within one mile range and clearly visible for anyone to see. Of the tribesmen who entered the picquet not a single one could have survived the devastating salvo that fell upon them a minute or so after. Yes, on this day too, the enemy suffered heavily, 400 casualties we were told. But our losses were also very severe. Our commanders were having their wish granted: the enemy were not only standing and fighting but attacking savagely in their fighting. Disdainful as to their own losses, they seemed determined to extract casualty for casualty.

What errors were we making that resulted in our own severe setbacks and losses? That question can be answered immediately. At Jandola all ranks had seen the many thousands of enemy who had crowded the long ridge. The congregated strength of the *lashkars* had been plainly discernible and, no doubt the Political Intelligence wallahs[4] had also given in their estimated figures. In view of that at least three battalions should have made the attack at Palosina on each commanding position in turn. Our piecemeal attacks caused our heavy losses. On both the right flank (Pioneer Hill Picquet) and the left flank (Mandana Hill) the enemy in strength far outnumbered our attacking troops. The two hills were not only extensive but their occupation was absolutely essential to the further advance of the Force into Mahsud country. As to the aggressiveness and courage of our enemy, we had the evidence of the Jandola battle to judge on. We had underestimated the capabilities of the Mahsud.

And because we had failed to judge correctly, the third day of our stay in Palosina camp had to be spent in refighting the two previous days' battles, attacking and occupying the Mandana Kach picquet. On this third day less opposition was encountered and the picquet was rebuilt correctly and so strongly wired, by two wide fences with aprons, that breaking through by the enemy would be impossible. Mandana and Pioneer picquets were situated practically opposite to each other so that the establishing of one greatly helped in the stabilizing and supporting of the other.

The day following the establishing of Mandana Kach, the Scouts were in camp for a day off and I climbed to the west ridge of the camp where the Indian mountain battalion was in action. Many thousands of yards away to the west could be seen a small plain and here crowds of tribesmen were gathered, probably discussing their next plan of action. By digging down the trails of his guns the Commanding Officer was able to set the extreme range necessary to harass the enemy, who could be seen through binoculars scattering to avoid the high explosives.

Not far beyond the camp and dominated by Mandana and Pioneer picquets was a lowish ridge which had a small hamlet of scattered huts. A recce party from the camp was on this ridge to consider our further advance to Kotkai, the next camp which, I was told, would be on the small plain the guns had been firing on. This party recovered the headless body of the Commanding Officer of one of the battalions. He had been killed in one of the battles and his body left out. In the search of the village the severed head was found in a hut in an earthenware pot. The troops were infuriated and the fact that no Mahsud prisoner was taken is probably due to the horrible tendency of the Mahsud to mutilate the dead. Some of the vile and disgusting mutilations they were guilty of are beyond description.

For the further advance of the Force some fresh infantry battalions were brought up to replace units that had suffered heavily in the Palosina engagements. These new units were all Gurkha battalions. The tough, brave little soldiers from Nepal, a hilly state to the north of India, were worthy of being pitted against the Mahsud, for the Gurkha is traditionally a courageous hill fighter and fleet of foot in the hills.

It is just as well that the Waziristan Frontier Force waited for their arrival before going on, because the toughest and fiercest battle of the campaign was to be fought out on the memorable day the column moved out of Palosina camp to advance up the Taki Zam, with Kot Kai as the objective. But between Palosina and Kot Kai was Ahnai (Asa Khan) about halfway. It was only thus far that we managed to fight our way on that day.

The fighting commenced at dawn as our leading troops moved up the valley. The enemy had chosen well their ground for this, their strongest opposition to our invasion of their country.[5] They had divided their combined numbers into three separate *lashkars*, one in front to stem our advance up the Taki Zam, and one on either flank to attack fiercely our route picquets, force them back into the close valley and thus have the column at their mercy to decimate. How nearly they achieved their intention can be gleaned from the fact that they did manage to drive in many of the route picquets and this forced our commander to sit tight that night where we were on the battlefield in the steep-sided nullah itself and a branch, precipitous-sided nullah which at that place entered the Taki Zam from the south and left, giving complete protection from sniping.

The battle raged in all directions and casualties mounted alarmingly, but our troops managed to hold back the attackers from gaining any position that would enable the enemy to fire into the nullah itself, where the vulnerable brigade train of animals which followed close on the advance were then herded for safety. Camels, mules, wounded and followers were packed like sardines that night into the small place, which providentially was available for us to use. The precipitous side of our emergency camp gave protection and picquets were closed in all around.

In the advance our Scouts were just behind the leading advance guard troops in the Taki Zam nullah itself, which varied in width from about 60 to 80 yards. The enemy were being pushed back slowly by our advancing soldiers until we passed the opening of the side nullah and arrived at a narrowish *tangi*.[6] Here a counter rush by a strong party of Mahsuds brought the advance to a halt and pinned down the vanguard. But in their counter-attack, the enemy sustained heavy losses and our Scouts, moving up through the vanguard with the Dogra Company of the Frontier Force Rifles, put a stop to any idea they might have had of driving through to the main body. Realizing this the survivors of the enemy counter-attack fled back a couple of hundred yards to safety round the next left-hand bend of the steep nullah. There were many large boulders bestrewing the bed of the nullah and I had barely taken up a position behind one with my orderly and one of my Militia officers, when he suddenly yanked me to one side out of danger. He had by chance glanced over his shoulder and spotted some Mahsuds immediately behind us, standing in a cave formed by an overhanging rock against the cliff side. For a second or two the three of us had been in full view of these Mahsuds and only about 10 yards from them. God alone had stayed them from shooting us and I was grateful. The noise of battle was all round us and the enemy shots would have passed unnoticed as, a few seconds later, did ours.

The advance of the Force was now halted and, a short while after, our Scouts were pulled out of the nullah to take up a defensive position on the flat ground immediately above and south of where we had been in the nullah. In this new position, which was about 80 feet above the nullah bed we protected the north-west front of the temporary camp being established in the flat bottom of the branch nullah bed. In our previous position we had had some protection from enemy fire on account of the high banks and the huge boulders which lay about, but up on the flat plain above there was no natural cover, not even a single bush or boulder, and no stones with which to build sangars. We lay there in the open, each of us trying to look as small as possible but feeling like sitting ducks for any damned Mahsud shikari to have a pot at. But luckily for us the main attention of the *lashkars* was directed towards our troops, who were precariously holding on to the north-east bank of the Taki Zam, and a working party of Pioneers, sappers and troops who, poor devils, had been put on to the unsavoury task of building a sangared picquet immediately on our right overlooking the stream. Their job would have been safe to carry out had our picquets been able to maintain the positions on the flatheads left and right, two prominent high features on our north flank. But those picquets had not been stabilised and the *lashkars* on our right and front were able to harass all our positions as they looked down on us. The enemy from the two hills I have mentioned poured volleys on to the working party building the camp picquet and within minutes they had fourteen men laid out. The building of that picquet was abandoned, and quite rightly so for even if the picquet had been completed, over-looked as it was, no occupying troops would have been able to remain in it for long.

The enemy now turned their attention to picking off individual stragglers of our withdrawing troops, who had been driven from their positions on the right. Some of these unfortunate lads, trying to escape the hail of bullets, were attempting to find a way back to the main body along a narrow path on the face of the north cliff, just above where we had been in the Taki Zam nullah. As they felt their way along the goat track the Mahsuds picked them off. It was terrible to see their bodies toppling down to the floor of the Taki Zam. We were powerless to help them. We could only lie where we were and watch with horror. Once the Mahsud snipers had accomplished that gruesome work there was nothing to prevent them from looking elsewhere for targets and their bullets now came in our direction.

By this time the afternoon was well advanced and an incident occurred which not only drew the attention of the Mahsuds away from peppering our Scouts, but also turned our own attention from our nasty predicament to that of others: a two-seater RAF plane came towards our position from the north-west after it had circled the two flathead hills. This was the first plane I had seen that had come to help in the operations and the first I had seen since my Mianwali flip. As I have explained earlier, the Taki Zam made a left-hand bend some distance to our front. After about a hundred yards it straightened out again, proceeding due west. This pilot, with great skill crash-landed his craft safely in the Taki Zam about 200 yards beyond our position on the plain. But from where we were we were not able to see into the nullah, and to rescue our Air Force friends about twenty-five of us Scouts ran forward to the far edge of the bend, from where the stranded airmen were seen struggling to get out of their cockpits. While two of our men, one an Indian officer and the other a sepoy, ran down the steep slope of the nullah to help back the two Britishers, who could barely walk for both were wounded, the rest of us took up positions and gave the two airmen and our two men covering fire to prevent the Mahsuds from rushing in to capture or kill the four men. But the enemy contended themselves with firing at them. With the greatest of courage under heavy fire our two lads helped the airmen along, half-carrying them struggling to get them up the slope of the nullah. Two Pathans risked their lives to save the lives of two strangers, Britishers.[7] The two rescued men were again hit by bullets and both my brave lads were also wounded. Others from our party ran down to help, and when all were safely on the level plain with us we rushed back to our original position and took the four wounded down to the field hospital. It was only by a miracle and God's grace that more of the party were not hit, for the Mahsuds were firing from two hundred to three hundred yards' range, and dust of the plain was being flicked up all round by vicious bullets. By this time darkness was approaching, and with dusk came respite from further attacks and bullets. The enemy were licking their wounds and we were licking ours. The *lashkars*, which had suffered at least 500 casualties in their persistent attacks, were in no mood or condition to continue the battle that night, and for all the troops it was just as well. The battle had lasted for twelve hours and more, and everyone was cold and weary, as well as hungry.

Because of our precarious defences, without sangars, wire or trenches, and lying out in the open expecting enemy rushes, we slept little that night. But nothing happened, no attack materialised and no sniping took place, all a sure sign of the severe knock that the tribesmen had taken.

Our own losses were heavy, 400 dead and wounded including fourteen British officers, most of them killed. The next morning, well aware of the proclivity of the Mahsud for stripping and mutilating our dead and even digging up their graves to loot the clothes and blankets they were buried in, a deep trench was dug under the cliff of the Taki Zam and then a good charge of explosives detonated to bring down a huge slice of the cliff to cover for ever the mass grave of our British dead. I missed being present at this sad, strange burial service because from dawn until late that day our Scouts were out for protection of the route towards Palosina. Our hundreds of wounded were being evacuated and our ration convoy and reinforcements were coming up. The

78

Brigade remained in that cramped but safe camp that day. Everyone was battle weary and no fighting took place.

That Ahnai encounter was the last big battle of the war but by no means the last fight. The tribesmen were not again able to concentrate such massive *lashkars* against us. We heard that the Wazir *lashkar* was fading out, due most probably to the adverse criticism levelled against them by their cousins the Mahsuds for their half-hearted actions. Besides that, by now the enemy must have suffered more than a thousand casualties in dead and many more wounded who would be unable to fight again. They surely knew that whatever resistance they could possibly produce, it could never be enough to stop our Force from getting to Kaniguram and Makin, the largest villages in the heart of their country. Their four or five great efforts had not been sufficient to stop our advance for more than two or three days, and they just had not the fighters to make any more like those. That they had fought well, with considerable courage and tenacity, had to be admitted by all. It was strange that the Mahsud always showed great punctiliousness in removing his dead from the battlegrounds during the night, yet left out the body of one man. Lying sprawling head downwards, on the face of the same big boulder behind which during the battle I had taken cover, was this corpse. Several times during the days that followed that battle I passed that rock when going on road-protection work, and the gruesome reminder of that fierce conflict was still there. Even the wild animals had given it a wide berth.

On those road-protection days after Ahnai, seeing those camels padding along with their leisurely strides, each with its precious burden of two sick or wounded soldiers, and each such convoy accompanied by a doctor and hospital orderlies, I thought how thankful one should be not to have been wounded and have to suffer for hours on end while being transported to some base hospital. In those days there were few motor ambulances and, in any case, there were no tracks suitable for motor transport. The best thing was to avoid getting sick or getting a bullet.

A couple of days after Ahnai the Brigade moved on to occupy the Kotkai plain. There was little opposition in establishing the camp picquets and the camp itself was well situated and easy to defend.

The scarcity of stones forced us to build our defensive perimeter wall with earth-filled sandbags and to get the necessary protection we dug down a couple of feet and built walls of filled sandbags.

After the strenuous time the Brigade had experienced since leaving Jandola, a few days of light work were welcomed. But even so, every little operation onwards towards our final objective resulted in fighting in varying degrees of intensity. A day or two after settling in to our new camp our brigade made a recce to the west as far as the next narrows, which were about three miles away up the Taki Zam. To cover this operation a long and large black-looking hill to the north of the valley was occupied by our troops. To look at, this formidable feature was like Pioneer Hill near Palosina. It was about three-quarters of a mile west of our camp and, with its eastern face sloping down towards Kotkai, it was therefore visible from camp.

For that recce our Scouts were sent out to occupy a group of mud-covered barren hills situated in a broad re-entrant to the south-west of the camp and only about 1,500 yards distant. Of course the commander did not know that there was a Mahsud village behind that group of lowish hills. If he had, he would surely have sent a battalion and not less than a hundred Militia Scouts to occupy the area. The planting of a day picquet on the hills we were sent to on that occasion struck me as unnecessary and unreasonable. It did not protect the route, which was the nullah bed of the Takizam; this was about 80 feet below the surrounding country and had steep sides. The positioning of a picquet just above the nullah would have been just as effective. As it was, and as you will read, our small body of Scouts, about eighty-five in strength (after deducting our wounded, sick and camp guard) was exposed to the gravest danger, quite avoidably.

We took the position without opposition and then I saw the Mahsud village. This was the first Mahsud village seen during the present operations and it was situated a couple of hundred yards away in a low valley. The Mahsuds would surely think that we were there to reconnoitre and perhaps attack, and would congregate to defend the area. My Indian officers were fully awake to our danger and we sent a group of men to occupy a lower knoll a short distance to our left front to watch out for any enemy move to concentrate below our main position. Our group would withdraw onto our hill if they were themselves threatened or saw our hill threatened.

Nothing happened until the withdrawal hour approached. In Frontier warfare this is the most critical period and the time when the fleet-footed tribesman can exact the maximum advantage, and therefore when our troops should be, more than ever, on the alert. The red flag of the rearguard of the withdrawing recce party appeared on the plateau above the Taki Zam in the distance, and I saw some of the distant picquets coming in and rejoining the main body of the rearguard. It was now the turn for the withdrawal of the picquet on the large black hill, which I have mentioned earlier. Obviously the Mahsuds also knew that, and the tragic event that followed occurred in full view because, from where I was sitting, I could see a large portion of the reverse slope as well as the slope towards the camp. As the rearguard drew level with the picquet I saw a huge, black, dense mass of tribesmen, at least 500 of them, moving with rapidity up the reverse slope of that big hill towards the summit. On the instant that our troops vacated the crest line to run down in their withdrawal, the enemy occupied it and not only commenced to fire into the backs of the soldiers but also, as they had done at Palosina, followed close on the heels of our men, intermingling with them, stabbing some, grabbing rifles, while they themselves were being covered by the fire of their own tribesmen on the crest.

Although I knew perfectly well, from what I had previously seen of the tactics of the Mahsuds in the other fights, what their manoeuvring and procedure in attack on a withdrawing force was, yet this was the first time that I had seen the whole system unfolding into tragedy for our troops before my very eyes. And what was happening there would happen to me and my Scouts, for the Mahsuds from that village would try the same game on us. But that tragedy on the Black Mountain slopes opposite was an immediate lesson and we did not fail to benefit from it.

That disastrous action delayed the withdrawal, and all delayed withdrawals due to enemy action are nerve racking for other troops waiting to be called in. When our guns, which were in action near the camp, commenced to pound the enemy on the black hill, they checked and withdrew knowing that the further they followed down the further they would have to retire under shrapnel bursts.

A counter-attack was made, and our troops returned to rescue the wounded and recover the dead. This took nearly two hours and in the meantime we had made our plan for our safe retirement to camp as there was no other picquet on our flank to help cover us back.

At last the RTR (retirement) signal came to us from the red flag of the rearguard, and in a minute our forward group went down to the plain below us with Percy, the Subadar Major and about a third of our men to give covering fire when our main picquet party started back from the crest. They moved fast and it wasn't five minutes before they were in position about 200 yards away and ready to fire on the crest of our hill as soon as we vacated. The rest of us now darted down, well extended, and at breakneck speed. What I had feared would happen took place. As soon as our forward group had moved, the enemy, seizing their opportunity as they were no longer watched, had rushed up to the dead ground below our crest line to come up to occupy it immediately after we left, and then to fire into our backs as we ran down. We had moved at terrific speed and were halfway down before the bullets of their firing began to kick up dust round us. My faithful orderly, a Sagri Uhattak, noticing the number of bullet splashes falling round the feet of his sahib, grabbed off my topee and replaced it with his own pugaree[8] as we raced along together. Perhaps the enemy were out of breath after their spurt uphill, or more likely the rapid fire being poured towards them by our covering party down below put them off their aim. At any rate nobody was hit, thank God, and we raced on back towards camp picking up our covering party on the way. The enemy soon had reason to regret their attack, for our guns opened up on them and they swiftly disappeared from sight – but not from the shrapnel from the howitzers which followed them and back down their side of the hill, where they erroneously thought and hoped that they would be safe from danger and shells as they were then out of view.

To enable the reader to understand how the above kind of enemy attack is possible, I shall try to explain a point or two. Most hills at the top are rounded and convex, some are quite bare of rocks, scrub and trees, others have plenty of natural cover in the way of

The Ahnai Tangi, the scene of bitter fighting against the Mahsouds in the 1919-20 campaign. (*Courtesy of the Estate of Major Willy Brown*)

Kotkai Fort. (*Courtesy of the Estate of Major Willy Brown*)

Splitoi Fort from
Khar Piquet.
(*Courtesy of the Estate
of Major Willy Brown*)

Hill formations
near Jandola.
(*Courtesy of the
Estate of Major
Willy Brown*)

A convoy on the road near Kotkai.
(*Courtesy of the Estate of Major Willy Brown*)

Sarwekai Fort from the inside. (*Courtesy of the Estate of Major Willy Brown*)

Holding a sangar near Ladha. The scout in the background is carrying a basket with four carrier pigeons. (*Courtesy of the Estate of Major Willy Brown*)

Gashting below the cliff at Sararogha. (*Courtesy of the Estate of Major Willy Brown*)

Mahsoud tribesemen.
(*Courtesy of the Estate
of Major Willy Brown*)

Howitzers in action.
(*Courtesy of the Estate
of Major Willy Brown*)

Mounted infantry. (*Courtesy of the Estate of Major Willy Brown*)

Typical Pathan villages with fortified walls and watch-towers.
(*Courtesy of the Estate of Major Willy Brown*)

Fording the Gomal River.
(*Courtesy of the Estate of Major Willy Brown*)

Post defence.
(*Courtesy of the Estate of Major Willy Brown*)

Last shoot with the
S.W.S. Six bulls and an
inner at 500 yards.
(*Courtesy of the Estate of
Major Willy Brown*)

A Brigade convoy on
the road near Sarwekai.
(*Courtesy of the Estate of
Major Willy Brown*)

bushes and broken ground. The most dangerous in defence are those which are devoid of all natural cover because the troops, taking up positions that would enable them to see the ground on the reverse and enemy slope, are then so far forward that they themselves are exposed to enemy fire. Consequently they keep back to avoid casualties. The enemy can then gather without being seen, make a sudden rush from quite close and, with their surprise attack, put the defenders at a disadvantage. This is undoubtedly what happened at Palosina and on this day on the big black hill.

Our brigade remained in Kotkai camp while the second moved through and on to establish camp at Sorarogha. To help them our brigade secured the route as far as the next defile. In this operation the Militia Scouts were again on the left flank, south of the Taki Zam, and the hill we were allotted to picquet was about a mile beyond the area we were last sent to. This hill presented no difficulties, neither in taking it nor in holding it. It was not only very rocky and broken but also had stunted, dried-looking bushes all along the crest line and down the far side. A company of Gurkhas went up to take the next hill on our side, about 500 yards further on, so we were in a good position to cover them and in the withdrawal to cover them down again.

The other brigade got through to Sorarogha without experiencing much opposition and as soon as their transport and camel convoy were through our Kotkai trooped commenced to withdraw. The Gurkha picquet was to retire before our turn came and to help them, in case they were followed up, our men were given an anticipatory fire order to be ready to fire on the vacated position to prevent or deter any enemy harassing the Gurkhas as they came away. They retired in two parties with a gap of about a hundred yards between. A British officer was with the last line as they came rushing down at good speed, for the little chaps are first class on a hill. The enemy went onto the crest of that hill within seconds and, although our fire kept them from following up they badly wounded one Gurkha soldier. He obviously called out to the British officer for help for that young officer halted dead in his tracks, rushed up the hill to where the wounded lad was lying, slung him over his shoulder and staggered down with his heavy burden. A really fine courageous act and I am glad to say that it was suitably rewarded by an immediate decoration. We had no trouble in getting back. No enemy could possibly have come up the reverse side of our hill without being seen, as we had posted forward groups hidden amongst the rocks and bushes.

Until our brigade moved up to Sorarogha, life in Kotkai remained peaceful except for sniping which sometimes continued for a couple of hours after nightfall. It was quite impossible to prevent this and, except for the nuisance value, hardly ever was any damage done. In the morning perhaps a camel or a mule would be found to be wounded or lying dead. These dumb and un-complaining animals never knew what had struck them in the night. They hardly ever moaned or gave any indication that they had been struck. If vulnerably hit they continued standing or sitting for a while, then would lie down and quietly expire. It was very seldom that a man was hit by sniping fire during the night for, not only were walls of filled sandbags built round every tent, but the space within each tent was dug down sufficiently to ensure complete protection from flying bullets. Steps led down into each tent and the flies were stretched tightly over the walls of sand-bags to carry away any rain that fell. Every permanent camp and permanent picquet was thoroughly protected in this way and had at least two double-apron fences of barbed wire surrounding it. The normal duties of units in camps on the line of communication consisted of running out close-protection troops almost daily to ensure the safe passage of the up and down convoys, and the safety of the parties carrying out the watering and rationing of the permanent picquets on the routes. Some of these picquets, situated in dangerous country, or distant from the main route, required a small-scale operation to cover their relief.

After a few days we moved on to Sorarogha with our brigade and from there helped the other brigade on to the next camp, Biaza Baghza. From about halfway to Biaza the country changed considerably, the hills being covered in small oak trees and in addition, the temperature became decidedly cold so that crossing and recrossing the stream in the early hours of the mornings was painful. Socks and *chaplies* froze hard and our feet felt like lumps of ice.

Sorarogha camp was situated on a plateau, even larger than the Kotkai plain, and the camp was extensive and comfortable. Strangely enough, the Mahsuds gave us very little trouble at this camp, perhaps because it was quite a distance from overlooking hills.

One morning, while walking outside the perimeter for some exercise, I saw a small Royal Flying Corps plane approaching. After it had circled once or twice it came down to land on our flat *raghza*, the surface of which was fairly level. It landed safely, but while taxiing to a halt a runaway mule got into its path and the plane, colliding into it, turned a complete somersault and lay with its wheels in the air. The unfortunate animal that caused the accident paid for it with its life. It died on the spot with a broken back. From under the plane crawled out two figures, the pilot and another officer, both obviously badly shaken but miraculously unhurt. The visitor, who had come to see the camp, turned out to be none other than our temporary commanding officer during the evacuation of Wana, Major G.H. Russell. In that disastrous withdrawal he had been badly wounded but had been carried to safety by his horse, a very beautiful little chestnut Arab mare which, although herself badly hit, was responsible for saving the life of her ever-grateful master.

Because of his accident and our picqueting duties it was not possible for me to see my previous CO, and in a day or two our Scouts were sent on their way to Piaza *raghza*, but were to be attached to the other brigade for the next advance, to Kaniguram not many miles further up the Taki Zam, and our final camp and objective. The camp at Piaza was also on a plain, but this *raghza* was covered in stones and was on a steepish slope. All the camp picquets were situated on scrub-covered hilltops, which gave snipers an easy opportunity to sneak up and worry the occupants. The 58th Frontier Force Rifles, to which we were attached for the next advance, were well dug in, and Percy and I were invited to join their Mess for that day and night. To get into the Mess tent we had to climb down about six feet. The CO of that battalion was a wise man, taking no unnecessary risks.

At a very dark and freezingly uncomfortable hour of the morning, following our arrival at Piaza *raghza*, the Force moved out of camp as quietly as our accompanying mules allowed. The commander had decided to advance up the narrowing valley of the Taki Zam as far as possible and as quickly as possible under cover of darkness, without sending up picquets. To this end the advance guard, to which our Scouts were attached, marched about a mile upstream in column formation. Suddenly and unexpectedly, the enemy gave those of us who were up forward the surprise of our lives. From some lowish hills on the left, volley after volley was let loose towards us in the dark. Although the enemy were not able to take aim at any definite target and had blazed away into the dark moving mass of our column, even so the violent racket caused by the volleys, plus the explosions of some hand grenades that were flung down towards us, were enough to be disconcerting. The troops withstood the surprise attack in quite an exemplary way and there was no panic. It was impossible to say in what strength the enemy were or what they would do next, however one thing was clear: surprise was no longer there and further advance required normal picqueting procedure. When I approached Major Jack Smyth VC MC, the advance guard commander close behind whom I was walking, our Scouts were immediately sent up to occupy the hill from which the fire was being directed at us. As far as I was concerned that was preferable to being cooped up in an unprotected defile. With all speed our Scouts took that hill with fixed bayonets, but there were no enemy there to greet us. They had fled, most probably because they did not know what was coming against them – a platoon or a battalion. A few hours later, when it was light enough to look round, we found the hilltop strewn with 'empties'. Usually the tribesmen collect any empty cartridge cases they can pick up, in the hope that one day they may be able to have them refilled.

That sharp but nasty affair ended our 'fun' for that day. The Force Commander, when he passed by in the morning light, decided that a permanent picquet be built on our position, so the remainder of the day was spent by us in protecting the working parties and lending a hand where we could, collecting stones, filling sandbags, clearing the area of scrub and putting up the wire fences. As the picquet was to accommodate a strong platoon of about forty soldiers, the perimeter required had to be about 40 to 50 yards and therefore the diameter about 15 yards. A section of

Madras sappers and miners was usually detailed to help build and wire each permanent picquet being constructed. These chaps were marvellously quick and efficient at their jobs, especially at putting up the wire. Their work was often dangerous and had to be carried out under sniping fire, but they carried on without seemingly worrying, and never left for camp and rest until their work was completed to the satisfaction of an officer. Our own brigade now moved on through, past the few route picquets put up by the Piaza *raghza* troops.

When the garrison for the picquet arrived with its many mule-loads of men's kits, cooking pots, water, reserve ammunition, canvas water tanks and a 160lb tent, the Indian officer in charge got down to detailing his guard and posting the day sentries. The wiring and clearing of all scrub within the vicinity of the picquet was completed, the tent put up, the water tank filled and all kit taken inside the picquet. As soon as the picquet commander reported that he was all right, the empty mules went down and I withdrew my men behind the hill, where we sat down to wait for our own brigade rearguard to come along and give me permission to move on to camp, a long way off.

By the time we got to Kaniguram that day there wasn't much time in which to get our camp in order before darkness fell. We were lucky in that we had not been allotted any perimeter to defend, so hadn't any wall to build. All our belongings had been unloaded on the small area of our campsite. Our camp followers and cooks had, I was glad to see, brewed tea for all and were getting on with preparing the night meal. It did not take us long to finish tea and put up our tents. Then came the long and hard job of digging down and making our tent walls. This kept us going well into the night. There was no letting up on this precaution for nobody knew how much sniping would take place and, to realize that one was safe behind a bulletproof wall gave comfort and peace of mind. It was bitterly cold at the high altitude we were now in but that night everyone was so tired that even the freezing could not keep sleep away.

Percy and I had good servants, both Punjabi Mussulmen who took everything in their stride and never once grumbled at the dangers and discomfiture they had to put up with in this severe Frontier campaign. They had cooked our meals, put up our tent and even helped to dig down the long narrow pits we unrolled our valises in. We shared an 80lb tent, large enough for living and feeding in. Our servants had a followers' tent, about 60lb in weight, and this also had to do for our Mess kitchen.

Having arrived in camp late, cold and tired out, we had little inclination to take a look round, but had caught a glimpse of Kaniguram village, almost a small town, which sprawled over the length of a long slanting spur that lay to the north of our camp, less than a mile distant. After a late supper of bully beef stew, tinned peaches with condensed milk and a cup of boiling hot coffee, Percy and I cast our weary bodies into our dugouts and rolled ourselves into our bedding to slumber.

As a general rule brigade orders for the next day were sent round to units early in the evening, but that night we did not get our copy until about eleven o'clock. Scrambling out of my warm bed and signing the receipt book for my copy, which the brigade orderly gave me by the light of a screened hurricane lamp, I glanced through and found to my joy that our Scouts were not detailed for any work the next day. We had been given a day to rest.

The Commanding Officer of a Frontier Force Rifles battalion had seen us in action at Ahnai and at Kot Kai, and now asked the Force Commander to permit our Scouts being attached to his regiment for the remainder of the operations. This was agreed to and from then on we received our orders for the next day's duty through the Adjutant of the 'Cookies',* the name by which that famous regiment was known throughout the Indian Army.

The class composition of the Regiment was the same as that of all the other Frontier Force battalions, i.e. one company each of Sikhs, Dogras, Punjabi, Mussulmen and Pathans. And because many of their Pathans are of the same tribe as ours, we were welcomed as brothers by the men. The 'Cookies' had suffered many casualties in the battles of Palosina and Ahnai and by attaching our small unit to them they were more or less brought up to strength again. For Percy, myself and our two servants it was a great relief that we no longer had to worry about Mess arrangements, for we were asked by the Colonel to join their large and comfortable Mess in which about twelve of us officers fed. Our servants only had to wait in Mess and were relieved of the trouble

* Coke's Rifles

of cooking our food as well as their own. The Commanding Officer of this regiment was a fine old pre-war officer of about thirty years' service and, besides being the Commandant, was the accepted 'Daddy' as well. Except for the CO and the second in command, also a pre-war officer, all the rest of us in the Mess were of about the same age and service, so were a happy crowd of youngsters together.

While in the Kaniguram area the Force occupied two camps. The first one we occupied was terribly cramped and quite the most uncomfortable I have ever been in. To make matters worse and almost unbearable in the constricted area, we experienced the first snowfall. About six inches of snow covered our small world during our third night in the Kaniguram. The hundreds of animals, which had to be taken out and brought back again two or three times every day for watering, turned all the camp roads into a sticky quagmire a foot in depth. For the first time in months I pulled on a pair of boots to get round in, for *chaplies* were wrenched off the feet and got lost in the horrible morass which, as the snow melted, got worse and worse. I feel sure that it was this state of affairs in the first camp that decided the Force Commander later on to move further north, when the *raghza* was not only more extensive but the surface firmer.

Everyone was glad that during this extremely cold spell the Mahsuds, who are never over-clad, retired into their caves and dwellings, and troubled us hardly at all. Our troops were all dressed in thick khaki serge jackets and plus fours, and had an extra issue blanket passed to each individual in the Force. Thick cardigans, a woollen muffler and woollen gloves, together with a balaclava pulled down well over the ears, helped everyone to combat the cold. To help keep our tent warm our orderlies turned an empty tin into a small oven and, as soon as the men's cooking was finished, would fill the tin with a few hot embers. This would in no time make the temperature of the tent bearable. One night, Percy returned from visiting some Mess where he had imbibed a little too well and, entering in high spirits, kicked the oven and the embers into my pit where I lay half-asleep. I was relieved to find that he was not too tight to help rescue his friend and his bedding from getting alight. My valise and a blanket or two never recovered from that incident and the holes burnt into them were a constant reminder until I passed the bedding on to my servant and invested in a new set.

One of the first operations our Scouts were sent on after joining our friends the 'Cookies' was the searching of Kaniguram. After the Battalion had occupied both ends of the long ridge our job was to go through, house by house, winkle out any tribesmen in hiding and have a general look round to report on the condition of the village which, although reported to have been bombed by the Royal Flying Corps, did not appear to have been badly damaged. There was one fairly high tower and two lesser ones, and I was curious to learn what these looked like from inside, how the occupants got to the top and how many rooms each had.

We commenced our search at the east end and my own part in the exploration ended there, at the first little dwelling which I entered. Looking round the small windowless room, my men and I found a bundle of rags, a few earthenware pots and one small *choola*, or cooking place. The room was really filthy with the floor covered in goat droppings, which led us to surmise that the owners of the house shared it with their flock. An urgent cry from my orderly drew my attention to my legs. I do not exaggerate when my eyes became riveted on a slowly advancing black mass of fleas climbing up my bootless, hose-encased legs. My men and I scampered out of that dwelling in no time and proceeded to de-flea each other frantically, in the hope that the attack would be brought to a stop before the vile insects became lost in the dark-coloured serge of our clothing.

The Mahsud and Wazir dwellings are built of clay which, when baked by the sun, become as hard as cement. The walls are constructed in layers, each clearly noticeable and about sixteen inches thick. Each layer is allowed to set dry before the next is built on to it. The tower is built of this same clay, with some rocks intermingled with it at the base. The first few feet of a tower are just solid clay and rocks, the lowest floor being above 8 feet above the ground, with the narrow single entrance situated well up for increased security. The bases of some large towers must be quite 20 feet square, tapering slightly towards the top, and these large ones have four rooms, with ladders leading from one floor up to the next. Most of the rooms are loopholed and the roof has a loopholed parapet high enough to give protection to a person sitting behind. Up here on the roof the defender can lie in wait for the opportunity to slay an enemy, a rival in love or a person against whom he has a blood feud.

On the whole the shacks in Kaniguram were very primitive in construction and, because of the severe cold of the winter months, few had windows. Little sun could enter the rooms and this most probably accounted for the swarm of fleas. How the people of Kaniguram could live in such filthy squalor with such poisonous and permanent companions was quite beyond our ken. This, the largest collection of habitations belonging to the Mahsuds, gave one the impression of being so poor, desperately poor, that it could not be worth destroying. Nor, as far as I know, was it ever destroyed.

I have to admit that from then on until we arrived at the west end, our search was not terribly thorough. No one in camp would have thanked us had we brought back millions of voracious vermin. We just went through the village, kicked open the doors of the houses and huts to make sure that no one was in hiding, and went on. After my experience at the beginning of the search my curiosity to examine the construction of a tower had also waned. The highest tower evidently belonged to a well-to-do Mahsud and no doubt about it, it was the one clean building we saw and had some large, well-ventilated rooms adjoining it. And on the flat roof he had collected about twenty or thirty dud bombs, dropped by the Royal Flying Corps. With these, by spreading them out at regular intervals, he had decorated the parapet of his extensive dwelling. The failure of these bombs to explode accounted for the almost complete lack of damage achieved by the Air Force. The roof of one small house had been blown open and the main tower had had a sizeable chunk removed from one of its corners.

Although the climate of this part of Waziristan was eminently suitable for the growing of fruit trees and vegetables, for it was almost the same as what we had in Wana but just 10 degrees colder in the winter, there was not the slightest sign of any sort of garden anywhere. Perhaps the Mahsuds, inveterate robbers that they were, realized the futility of growing any product which stood a good chance of being purloined by their friends during the hours of darkness. And this, of course, in turn might lead to a quarrel and then a blood feud.

After going through the village we moved up the slope to where a company of the Regiment was building a permanent picquet to cover future advances and withdrawals during our strikes at far-afield towers and villages. This, in case the Mahsuds continued to be adamant in their refusal to come to terms and hand back to us all the arms and weapons they had taken and captured since the evacuation of Wana. The Force was now within easy reach of the high towers owned by most of the prominent *maliks* (leaders) and the commander intended to bring full pressure on them, and to insist on their accepting responsibility for the behaviour of their own clans.

The picquet that was under construction lay in full view of a long ridge running down to the *raghza* parallel to the Kaniguram spur, and from here sniping was troubling the building parties at about six to eight hundred yards' range. A few men had been hit and, as we arrived, the British officer commanding the company took a bullet through the stomach. After applying a first-aid bandage we sent him down to camp on a stretcher under an escort of a section. He had not seemed to be in much pain and he and I chatted for a minute or so before they carried him down. Smith was a tough chap and in a few weeks he was back again with the 'Cookies', having been right down to the base hospital in Rawalpindi.

The sniper continued to worry us and make life precarious, and we set some Pathans on to spotting any indication that would give away his position. Sure enough one of our men saw a move-ment behind a large, darkish-looking stone, and when through binoculars we glued our eyes on the area, the sniper showed a slight movement as he brought up his rifle to take aim. An Indian mountain battery was in action a few hundred yards back and we sent a posse of men to the gunner officer to point out the exact position of that sniper. The very first high-explosive shell he directed to that large dark stone struck where it was meant to and ended that troublemaker's attentions.

A day or two later it was the turn of our Scouts to construct a permanent picquet on a wooded ridge to the south of the camp and about a mile away. A company of the 'Cookies' were further along to the west on the same long ridge to protect us from sudden attack. Right from the start both our parties were subjected to sniping fire and a few men were wounded. One of the men hit was in a forward group sent out by the other company and the Commander, Felix Williams, went forward himself to bring back his wounded lad under fire. A very courageous act.

Building a picquet under fire, even long-range sniping fire is a nasty business. Sooner or later someone remains in view and stationary long enough for the sniper to align his sights and press the trigger. And even if the bullet misses its mark, it is going to be by a slight margin. To have a carefully fired bullet just missing one's ear leaves that organ completely deaf for about five minutes and the nerves of that human target agitated while he ponders his narrow escape. Because of the accurate sniping fire the south portion of the wiring for the picquet was left until semi-darkness, blanking out the sniper's aim. The Sappers completed the wire and our Scouts cleared the scrub and bushes. The picquet was not occupied by the garrison until fairly late that night when the company, the Sappers and our Scouts withdrew to camp escorting the mules that had brought up the kits and stores of the picquet.

As I have mentioned earlier, the first Kaniguram camp was a dreadfully cramped one and so, when the commander moved the Force to the *raghza* a mile or so away to the north, everyone was delighted. Besides being located on a large flat plain with a firm surface, the camp was now further away from commanding features and therefore less troubled by snipers during the night. But even so, all units had strict orders to complete all their cooking and have lights blanketed before dark. This was the best camp we had built and soon all units were well dug down, warm and comfortable for our longish stay in the area.

That day a Gurkha battalion had moved out at dawn to cover the west and dangerous flank during the occupation of the new camp, the west boundary of which was a nullah about 50 yards wide and 20 feet deep. Changing camp took all day and it was not until near dusk that the Force Commander considered it safe for the covering Gurkhas to come in. The Mahsuds were clearly waiting for this opportunity to show their prowess in the fading light. Amongst the stunted oak that were scattered on the steep *raghza*, cut in places by some nullahs which gave them approach lines, they followed up closely, inflicting several casualties and forcing the rear lines of our troops to halt and counter-attack to evacuate their wounded. Now developed the same type of battle which I had witnessed at Jandola on our first day with the Force. Our howitzer battery, ideal for close support, was in action on the west edge of the camp and when the counter-attack was launched, the four guns were firing at enemy not more than five or six hundred yards from camp. I was standing behind the line of British-manned guns and was able to watch distinctly the shells from the muzzles of the guns for the first few hundred feet of their trajectory, until their shrapnel was discharged to burst amongst the tribesmen who were checked in their attack. But as soon as the withdrawal after the counter-attack commenced, the Mahsuds again pressed hard upon the rear of our men to within a hundred yards of the perimeter. Darkness was fast approaching and it was soon difficult to distinguish between enemy and friend. The troops came back in short rushes, parties covering each other as they moved. The howitzers continued firing until the Gurkhas were back in camp and the short but very fierce battle then ended. This was the nearest approach to an attack on a camp of the Force that had occurred.

Many dead from that battle had been left out on the plain to be brought in the following morning. Our Militia Scouts, with other troops, moved out at daybreak to collect and send back the dead, a pathetic and grim job. As had been seen so many times before, the bodies had been stripped of all clothing and had been badly mutilated. This mutilating of our dead left such a feeling of hatred in the hearts of our little Gurkha friends that they swore revenge, and this they were able to get not many days later.

This serious encounter made it clear that the Mahsuds were not as yet inclined to come to terms, and so a strong Force moved out to the north-west in the direction of the Makin Maliks' villages and towers, or fortified dwellings. The main objective of this operation was a particularly high and well-built tower that was the property of an influential Makin chief. The destruction of this fine tribal fortress would perhaps encourage the leaders to persuade their hotheads from further provocations, and so save their own habitations from retaliations by the Waziristan Field

Force, which was now in a position to strike at their distant villages that up to now they had thought safe and impregnable.

The Force moved out in the very early hours of the morning with a pale moon attempting to shine through a screen of thin clouds, giving the earth a ghastly pallor. Our Scouts were with the vanguard up in front, being led by a Political *Tahsildar*[9] who knew the ground. We were proceeding cautiously and in dead silence, with small groups out on either flank and had been on the move for about an hour when the silence was shattered by an agonizing cry for help from our left front. As we were leading the column it was not possible to stop and hold up the operation for other troops were close behind us, but I sent a runner to find out what had happened, and to follow up and report. After a few minutes he returned to say that one of our Scouts moving on the left of our flank group had fallen over a nullah cliff, about 15 to 20 feet deep. At his cry the man's brother, recognizing it, ran to his brother's help and he too, not seeing the nullah in the strange light, went over the same cliff. The colour of the ground we walked on and the colour of the bottom of the nullah merged without showing any break, and this accounted for the very strange accident. The two brothers lay together, both with broken limbs.

Leaving a couple of men to inform the field ambulance with the Colonel, and to look after the injured lads, we continued on our way slowly for another hour or so until, just before dawn, the tower began to loom up in the distance. We now came to a halt, our job was over and the battalion which was to cover the engineers, who had to prepare charges for blowing the huge tower, went through to occupy the ground beyond and on the flanks. The tower and the habitations that always surround one were found deserted and so there was no delay in the sappers getting on with their work of laying their charges to destroy the property. It did not take them long to complete their preparations, bury their explosives and lay the fuses. All was ready as dawn broke and the sun appeared over the Razmak Hills. The covering troops withdrew and, when level with the tower, the sappers lit their fuses and all ran back to a safe distance to watch the buildings and tower disintegrate.

When the charge in the base of the tower ignited there was not much of a bang, just a muffled explosion. The solid base of the tower shattered outwards in all directions, then the noble edifice, left standing without support for a fraction of a second sank down into the rubble of the surrounding buildings, breaking into a thousand pieces. As the dust cleared the remains, with hundreds of rafters sticking out in all directions, looked like a defunct porcupine. Back in camp I went along to the field hospital to find out about my two men who had fallen into the deep nullah during the night. I was surprised to learn that both had already been evacuated the same morning by the down convoy after being attended to. Some weeks later I heard that both brothers had been given injury pensions. They had been seriously hurt.

Perhaps because of the surprise of our night advance no opposition had been met, either going or during the withdrawal, and the column had got back into camp before ten in the morning. And so after a late breakfast everyone was able to make up for the loss of sleep caused by the previous night's operation.

The political powers with us continued to report no signs of submission on the part of the Mahsuds and therefore further persuasive and strong action was decided upon by our commander. The first of these was the establishing of a very strong company permanent picquet to the north-west of the camp and not far from where the recently destroyed tower had stood. This was carried out as a night operation and again the Mahsuds, taken by surprise, were not in a position to put up any opposition or follow up the withdrawal. In this picquet there were two British officers, one of them a forward observation officer from the howitzer battery. As the position was on a high spur, this gunner subaltern was able to send back to his battery, in action in camp, information about movements of tribesmen and their flocks and herds far to the west and on the slopes. This harassing fire of the guns forced the Mahsuds to evacuate their warm homes and take refuge in the bleak hills.

A week or so after the picquet had been built, the young forward observation officer, while directing the fire of the guns, was peering through a rather largely made loophole when a sniper, who had probably crept up close under some cover, shot the lad dead. This sad incident cast a gloom over the whole camp, for not only was he most popular with all in the Force, but also because, since the Ahnai battle, no British officer had been killed. As far as I can remember this boy of nineteen was our last British officer casualty.

Another company picquet was built far to the south-west and in a very isolated position at the end of a high wooded spur. This position was also intended to open up and give freedom of action to a large inhabited area, which up to this time the Force had not operated over. The operation was again carried out as a night attack, with our Scouts moving up and then along the wooded ridge until we arrived at the place where the picquet was to be built. We had left camp just after midnight and arrived, after going slowly through the thick jungle at about two-thirty in the dark, early morning. Our part in this scheme was to protect the picquet construction parties and also help in clearing the vicinity of the picquet to give the garrison a clear field of fire. Gurkha troops moved along below the spur in the valley, guarded by us on their left and by another Gurkha battalion on their right. When we halted at our position the Gurkhas also waited below us, so as to make their attack on the Mahsud habitations at dawn. Everything went like clockwork, the construction and clearing making good headway, considering we had to work in the dark and as quietly as possible. To show how silently the men carried out their jobs, a large congregation of Mahsuds, who were gathered a few hundred feet below where my men had taken up forward positions, were completely unaware of what was going on above them and sat round an enormous log fire which they continually replenished, making the flames and sparks shoot into the air like fireworks. I expect they were planning some attack, not knowing that we were doing the same. Of course we wanted to leave them in ignorance until the picquet was completed, or when dawn broke and the Gurkhas went in to the attack. As it was difficult collecting stone in the darkness, most of the building up of the wall was done with earth-filled sandbags, the earth being found from the excavated interior. By the time dawn came most of the hard work was completed and only the finishing touches remained to be attended to. The wiring of the two double fences was made particularly strong on account of the isolated position of the garrison.

The Gurkhas moved forward at daybreak and surprised the Mahsuds in the attack they launched. Some of them were still at the bonfire warming themselves when they were fired at. The enemy at once tried to come up the hill and so get above the Gurkhas, but they bumped into our Scouts and had to retire down and across the valley to the shelter of the distant hills, where they sat and watched the Gurkhas dealing with their village. In the meantime the Pathan company of the 'Cookies', who were to occupy the picquet, arrived under their company commander, Smith, who had rejoined the Battalion as soon as his wound had healed.

The shells of our two batteries had followed the enemy as they retreated into the mountains and scattered behind rocks to avoid the bursts, but through my binoculars I could see small parties collecting and then breaking off to the north and south. I felt sure that they were biding their time till the long withdrawal back to camp would give them the opportunity to wreak revenge for what the Gurkhas were doing to their houses. Smith and his *jawans* occupied the picquet, unloaded all their stores and filled their four or five canvas water tanks. Two tents, joined together, were erected, guards and double sentries posted and the working parties departed for camp taking the unloaded mules with them. It was not yet 10.00 a.m. and as the move back to camp would not be starting until 11.00, my friend and I sat concealed in a big sangar and watched the Gurkhas at their work below us.

In the withdrawal we had to protect the Gurkhas' southern flank and see that no enemy sneaked in between the high, lengthy ridge of the spur we were on, or the bottom of the same spur, to fire down at the Gurkhas. There was little danger of the Mahsuds attacking our Scouts as we went back slowly in parties because of Smith's strong picquet behind us. From where I was moving I was able to watch the tactics of the Mahsuds who, no sooner had the Gurkhas commenced to retire, began to follow up in small groups, using every small depression, nullah or clump of bushes to gain distance. They kept out of effective range of our Scouts and the picquet just built, so the withdrawing rearguard of the Gurkhas had only a limited and fairly narrow strip of dangerous going to look after, their north flank being secure as I have mentioned earlier. Their parties withdrew with great skill and carefully located covering sections kept the tribesmen at a good distance, however they continued to follow, waiting for the Gurkhas to make a mistake. But instead of finding and taking advantage of a Gurkha mistake, they themselves, abandoning caution in their attempt to cause casualties and hold up the withdrawal (which is always their aim), fell into a meticulously conceived and laid *chapao* and suffered the loss of a complete follow-up group. This dampened their ardour and they gave up as suddenly as they had begun. The Force arrived back at camp without having had a casualty, and so ended a perfectly planned and executed operation.

For the next few days, night after night operations such as have been described were carried out in different directions, the Mahsuds never knowing where the next blow would fall. The strain of these freezing cold night operations was beginning to tell and be felt by all troops, but the Force Commander was determined to continue the pressure and keep the enemy on the run, and soon they began to show signs that they were getting rattled. No doubt they were being influenced by their wives and dependants who, driven up into the mountain fastnesses with their flocks and herds, were feeling the extreme bitter cold of the wind-swept crags.

Peace feelers began to arrive from some Maliks through the Political Agent, but there was no sign of accepting or listening to any until all the terms laid down by the Force Commander were accepted en bloc by all the leading Maliks, none being omitted, and every one of these Maliks would be expected to present himself at a *jirga*, or gathering, to be presided over by the Commander of the Force. Pressure was maintained. This may appear brutal, but in casting a thought back on what has been said regarding the brutalities shown to Indian villagers by Mahsud and other tribal raiders during the preceding year, perhaps it will be accepted that because of the tribes' savage and vicious attacks on quite innocent folk, firm action was essential. Every endeavour had to be made to impress upon the trans-border recalcitrants that their ways required changing.

Eventually all the terms were accepted and so the date for the *jirga* was fixed. On the morning of that day a large semi-circle of chairs was arranged on the *maidan* outside the north perimeter of our camp. When all the Maliks and elders of the Mahsud tribes had arrived and had been checked by the 'Politicals', they squatted down to complete the circle. Surrounding this was another circle, much larger than the first, a guard of a hundred or more Indian soldiers, Sikhs, Punjabi Mussulmen, Gurkhas, Dogras and Pathans, all standing with loaded and fixed-bayoneted rifles. Some of them wore very grim expressions, for weren't these Mahsuds their hated *dushman*, or enemy? And, for sure, some in the guard had lost a brother, cousin or good friend, perhaps whose body he had later seen horribly mutilated, a vile act committed against all religions and moral teachings. For some of them there would have been nothing they would have welcomed more than a little incident, rudeness or act to give them an excuse to bury their bayonets in the bodies of these detestable people.

But the Maliks gave their assurances in open *jirga* and the gathering of the leaders of those cut-throats passed off without any nasty incident. After the terms had been accepted, the demanded number of rifles and other arms surrendered in a huge pile and checked, and the requisite number of hostages handed over for detention in India as a guarantee of the Mahsud tribes' honest acceptance of the terms, the Maliks and elders were escorted some distance from the camp and sent off by the political people.

[Editor's note: The life of a Frontier solider was not all warfare and punitive expeditions. Cumming was passionate about shooting, or *shikar*, and would never miss an opportunity to ride into the badlands in search of game. Whenever he was in Peshawar, during that period of relative calm between the end of the Third Afghan War and the outbreak of the Second World War, Cumming became a familiar face on the dance floor of the Peshawar Club and at the sumptuous banquets in the Officers' Mess. These were the trappings of English life transposed to a colonial outpost, yet Cumming was quite satisfied to enjoy his leisure pastimes in India. Much to his surprise, after ten years' service on the Frontier, he was offered a full year's furlough in England. Then, to his dismay, he found life at home a bore, with nothing to do but spend his savings, so after eight months he packed his bag and booked passage to Aden to join his battalion. The experience of serving on the North-West Frontier developed into a love-hate affair for most of the men who served there, with the balance tipped heavily on the love side. It must be remembered that British officers fought alongside as well as against the Pathans, whose heroism in battle and determination to defend their homeland inspired deep respect. There was an extraordinary mutual respect on both sides of the battlefield. This is epitomized by an episode that took place after the 1908 campaign against the Zakka Khels, when the tribal leaders came to tender their submission to the British officer in charge, who happened to be the celebrated Frontiersman, George Roos-Keppel. As the maliks crowded round their adversary, one old grey-beard stepped forward to ask, 'Did we not fight well, sahib?' Roos-Keppel looked him straight in the eye and replied, 'I wouldn't have shaken hands with you unless you had.']

Chapter 4

Getting to Know Thy Enemy

There is an old Pathan proverb: 'Pathan honour is like a stainless blade that will not tarnish in the torrents of time.' However, a Mahsud cannot be relied upon to keep his word and agreement. Everyone knows this and that some sections of the tribesmen would not fail to take advantage of any lapse in security precautions that might become evident and inviting. The time was approaching when we would keep our part in the contract and withdraw from their territory and that, as always, would be a severe period of temptation for the diehards in their midst. Because success had crowned all the night operations the Force had undertaken while in Kaniguram, our commander decided to carry out the initial part of the withdrawal from our camp to Piaza *raghza* as secretly as possible during the dark early hours of the morning, and that at any rate, the bulk of the main body should be out by dawn.

To try to maintain some secrecy, or at any rate leave the Mahsuds in doubt as to the exact day of the departure of the Force, some picquets, not necessary for the protection of the camp, were left out with orders to come in under their own steam during the night. One of these was the Pathan Company picquet under Smith, out in the blue to the west. This was the only one that presented a real problem, as the others had not far to come in. The 'Cookies' Pathans not only had a long way to withdraw but the route was beset with snags, and besides this difficulty it was known that during the night Mahsuds used to occupy the caves below the picquet on the far side – in other words, many enemy would be in the vicinity.

The big job of packing up the camp was started after darkness had fallen, and the troops who were to be actually involved in the rearguard operation of the evacuation moved out with mules to relieve the garrisons of the camp picquets, who then rejoined their units in camp.

Our Scouts were again to operate on the south flank of the withdrawal. Leaving half a dozen men behind to help the followers of our unit pack up our small camp and load the mules and camels, the remainder moved out with some mules to occupy the ridge occupied by the picquet that our Scouts had built not many weeks before. We climbed up slowly in the darkness, arriving safely after an hour's walk. We relieved the garrison of the picquet, who were already packed up. They loaded their tents and other belongings on the animals and went off down the hill, while my men deployed along the long ridge with two groups down the far side. As we still had a couple of hours to wait before dawn, some of the men were employed in cutting long leafy branches from the stunted oak, and with these we made a long screen, planting them in the ground from the picquet and back for a hundred yards. The intention was to keep the enemy in ignorance as to whether we were still in occupation of the area when the time for retirement came. To take every conceivable precaution to prevent having a man hit during our withdrawal was uppermost in my mind. Many tragedies had resulted, after casualties sustained during that critical period of rearward movement, but up to this time, thanks be to God, we had not had a man killed, although we had had several wounded.

From our position on the ridge no indication of the packing up of that huge camp was apparent. Not a single fire or lamp was visible, the striking of the tents, rolling up of kits, the loading of the mules and camels, all were carried out in darkness, and the main body of the column was ready and assembled outside the perimeter of the camp by dawn. Not a shot had been fired and, as the first signs of dawn approached, the animals moved off down to the Taki Zam valley, protected by its own advance and convoy guard. The troops forming the rearguard of the withdrawing force were left behind in command of the area.

The systematic and carefully co-ordinated calling in of the picquets and parties of troops from their covering positions of the camp area was started once the main body was out of range and well on its way down the route. With the main body proceeded detailed units to take over from the route-permanent picquets, and spare animals to carry their kits. All the outlying picquets, except the Pathan company's distant one, had reported in safely during the night, and as our Scouts were on the south flank of the withdrawal, we kept an anxious eye open to locate our friends as they passed by. We could not retire from our ridge until we were assured that they were back inside the protection of the rearguard, and naturally expected to see them come in on the safe side of the valley where we were in position to give help if needed. When they did not appear and a messenger was sent to the rearguard commander telling him about the non-arrival of that picquet, he held up the retirement and sent back to the Commanding Officer of the 'Cookies' to enquire. After a delay of fifteen minutes news came to us that the picquet was in OK and the withdrawal proceeded. Apparently the picquet had withdrawn and had just reported in a few hundred yards lower down the route.

Once the covering troops were clear of the vacated camp area hundreds of tribesmen, many of them armed, swarmed on to the area to see what they could glean from the remnants and rubbish left behind by the troops. Because no firing had taken place so far these people were left unmolested by our rearguard and the guns. As the red flag passed our picquet area we were given the signal (RTR) to retire. Under cover of the screen we had put up, our men sneaked back quietly and when well away from the sangar we raced along the top of the spur, covered by our successive groups which we picked up as we drew level with them. We dropped into the valley where the spur ended and reported in safely at the headquarters of the rearguard. However, we were not finished with rearguard work yet. We were instructed to proceed back to the point where rearguard duties were taken over from the Kaniguram troops by a rearguard formed to operate back on the Piaza *raghza* by that camp's troops. So we collected and moved along at speed to report to the Commanding Officer of the 58th Frontier Force Rifles from Piaza. I had met him before, of course, the night we had spent in Piaza on our way to Kaniguram. He kept our Scouts in his rearguard reserve. This meant that we would be amongst the last to get into camp that evening.

Up to the time that the Razmak-Kaniguram rearguard handed over its duties to the Piaza Roghza rearguard, the Mahsuds had not troubled the retirement in any way, but from then on groups of them followed up, some occupying vacated picquets, and harassed the further retirement of the Force. The assurances given by the Mahsuds in open *jirga* at Kaniguram were already forgotten. The enemy had not done this while our rearguard was still in the Kaniguram-Razmak area as they knew full well that if they had, our guns would have opened up on the crowds of them invading the vacated camp. They waited until we were well out of range before attacking.

We knew that malcontents and irreconcilable individuals amongst the Mahsuds would surely give trouble, and that whatever agreements had been entered into by their Maliks it would make little difference to them, for they were a law unto themselves. The chance of picking up the rifle of a slain soldier was an irresistible temptation to many of these hotheads. But by now, after many months of fighting and experience in the ways and tactics of our enemy, our troops were confident in their ability to repay them as much, if not more than they gave.

The rearguard commander of the Piaza troops kept our Scouts near his headquarters by the red flag. We all moved along in parties on either side of the Taki Zam nullah, where rocks and bushes gave quite considerable cover whenever a halt was called to bring in a route picquet. By keeping clear of the open bed of the river, we avoided the unnecessary risk of a casualty. Everything went smoothly and the picquets came in at great speed, giving the tribesmen no chance to make surprise close-in rushes. In fact they were kept at a distance by carefully placed covering-fire parties of troops. But they followed up, sniping at the withdrawing picquets and the rear lines of the rearguard, until we arrived within the safe circle of Piaza *raghza* camp picquets.

Back in camp, in the Mess that night, my friend Smith, the Pathan company commander, told me the exciting details of his company's withdrawal from the outlying picquet, explaining why he had used a different route to the one we all expected him to take in his withdrawal. Apparently the Mahsuds of that area had tumbled to the fact that the picquet would be withdrawing. Of course, they couldn't possibly have known for certain or that a covering force would not be going out to help them in. At any rate, during the evening they had taken up a blocking position across the long ridge the picquet was on and at about a hundred yards from the sangar. This had become known to the picquet after sundry suspicious noises had been heard coming from the enemy *chapao* and a couple of stalwarts had verified the fact by sneaking out and spying carefully through the thick undergrowth. A conference was then held by Smith and his men when it was decided that the best way of getting away secretly was to avoid using the main exit of the picquet and the spur route, and instead, with great care and absolute silence, open out a very narrow exit in the opposite wall of the sangar, cut a few of the lower strands of the wire fencing and so creep out and down towards the enemy village on the west side of the hill. They proceeded to carry out their plan and after a couple of hours' careful work, everything was ready for the garrison to move off. The openings in the wall and under the wire were just large enough for men to crawl through carefully in single file and the whole company, one by one, left the picquet. After going about a hundred yards beyond and below the picquet through the bushes, they assembled and checked up their sections and platoons. Then, wheeling left, the men went down into the thick jungle to the south of the ridge before moving along eastward, keeping well down and away from the crest of the ridge. They all went along at a snail's pace in the dark to ensure keeping in touch with each other and moving silently, their greatest difficulty the maintaining of the correct direction in the dark through the jungle. Pathans are good at finding their way at night and by going carefully, they made no mistake. Their careful, accurate and silent progress through the night was surely proved by the fact that although more than a hundred men passed by the two groups of my men, whom I had posted quite far down the south slope of the ridge which we had held during the night and up to the withdrawal, no indication of the Pathan company's movement was heard by them. It was just as well that our men had not seen or heard the Pathan company finding their way along. If they had perhaps firing would have broken out between friends. The Company, after passing below our position, still had a half mile to go before they emerged through the re-entrant where our spur ended into the Taki Zam valley. Covering this distance safely they joined the main body and sent back the All Clear to the rearguard, altogether a really fine bit of work and the initiative showed by Smith gained him the immediate award of the Military Cross, surely a well-earned decoration.

The Force came back down from the Taki Zam in stages and without any more attacks by the tribesmen until we came to Kotkai, where the column halted for a few days. South of the camp, and only two or three miles away, lived a sub-tribe of Mahsuds who had consistently given trouble, both before and after the Kaniguram *jirga* when peace terms had been accepted by them. Besides this the political people had some other counts against them and so the column was detailed to punish them by destroying their village.[1] I had reason to believe that these Mahsuds were the same crowd who attacked our picquet on that day at Kotkai and shot us up as we withdrew, luckily for us without causing a casualty.

The Scouts had a day off in camp on the day of the operation and the Commanding Officer of the 'Cookies' asked me if I would like to command their Dogra Company on that occasion.[2] I readily agreed for I had a tremendous admiration for those little hill men from Jammu and Kangra. They had fought alongside my *jawans* in the big battle of Ahnai with great bravery.

Moving out of camp in the dark, our force arrived at the village before dawn. After putting up some picquets on the route to cover our withdrawal later on, within an hour our troops covering the destruction of the buildings had taken the hills to the east, south and west of the area. Quite clearly the inhabitants were taken by surprise, for we saw them rushing out of their dwellings and driving their camels, goats, sheep and donkeys up the valley that led west. Many women accompanied this exodus. The troops did not fire at anyone as we had orders not to unless fired at.

The hill the Dogra Company was detailed to take and hold was long, rocky and covered in dry-looking bushes, so there was lots of cover and the enemy would have no opportunity of attacking us without our observing him coming all the way. Therefore there was little chance of him taking this risk. However, after an hour on the position snipers started to fire at us from one of two distant positions but, as the men had built sangars behind which they crouched, only a lucky enemy shot through a head was possible and this would require pretty accurate shooting at three or four hundred yards. Therefore we were not unduly perturbed. One of the snipers was firing from a flat bit of country slightly below and to the left of the ridge we occupied. It took me quite a long time to locate the firer, which I eventually did. What had made me take a special interest in this Mahsud was that a small twig, snapped off by a bullet, had fallen down, past my face, into my lap as I sat behind my sangar under a bush. I picked up the twig and on examining it I realized that this sniper had been firing at me but his bullets had been going well above. He had badly overestimated his range. Borrowing my orderly's rifle I waited for him to emerge slowly for his next attempt. The man was hiding behind a large solitary log and I had seen his movement when he slid up his rifle over the log to take aim. I reckoned that he was 300 yards from us, so I set my sights at 250, knowing full well that the bullet would penetrate the dry wood even if it hit three inches below the top edge of the log. I hadn't long to wait and was ready when his rifle, then his head, appeared gradually and very slowly he took aim. I did not wait for him to fire that shot but pressed the trigger of my gun. The quickness with which that sniper disappeared with his rifle showed that my bullet, if not having found its mark at any rate frightened the life out of him. He did not appear again and if alive obviously disliked being fired at as much as I did.

The field engineers had in the meantime been preparing the only tower for destruction by blowing it up. Working parties of men had tried to destroy some of the buildings by pulling or pushing over the walls, but this had proved to be a most difficult and laborious undertaking, and it had taken a whole platoon of *jawans* a full half hour to shove one over. As it was not feasible to blow up all the houses, there being too many of them, it was decided to burn the roof of each dwelling. The replacing of these would take long and cost the owners quite a lot because the pine tree rafters had to be brought from miles away from the Marwaties.[3] From here we were way forward and to the west. One of our Dogras drew my attention to a large mass of Mahsuds moving east and up towards a position occupied by a company of another unit. Luckily our Dogra signallers were able to get in touch with the headquarters of the unit and I sent a message informing them of the danger in store for the picquet. We soon saw covering fire parties taking up positions to help the threatened men.

The tall tower was blown out sideways and collapsed in a cloud of dust. Men went round the dwellings setting fire to the roof of each house with the aid of torches, after a hole had been made in each roof to assist the draught to finish the work commenced by the torches. Then the engineers and working parties fell back to the main body before the picquets began to be called in from the covering positions they held. We were one of the first to withdraw and had no trouble in getting back safely to the red flag of the rearguard. The picquet that was threatened also got away safely, but the tribesmen were seen on the vacated hill a few seconds later and were duly punished by our howitzers waiting to blast them off the top.

The withdrawal to camp, after the costly experiment of the Mahsuds to inflict casualties, was carried out without further incident. The enemy were too subdued by their double trouble to follow up. And so ended the last fight I was present at during the Scouts' stay with the Waziristan Field Force. A day or two later our Scouts were recalled to our headquarters, which had by now moved to our old Militia post, Murtaza. I had felt it a great honour to have had the privilege of serving with the famous 'Cookies' and in the last encounter with the enemy to have been given the chance to command one of their companies. What a magnificent crowd the 'Cookies' were – from the weather-beaten dear old Commanding Officer to the youngest subaltern, they had received us all into their happy family and showed us the greatest kindness. After saying farewell to our friends we went down the Taki Zam in stages, Palosina, Jandola, Khirgi, and across the rock-strewn Girni *raghza* that lay between Khirgi and Murtaza.

Many changes had taken place in the South Waziristan Militia while Percy, I and the Scouts had been away with the Waziristan Field Force. We were reforming for another big job that began to loom up before us in the not-too-distant future. Teddy Davis, our old commanding officer, had left to rejoin his active battalion to take over command, and Barker, Percy and I were now the only British officers of the old Wana crowd still serving. Hundreds of fresh recruits, mostly Khattaks, Bangash and Yusafzais,[4] were enlisted and strenuous training and parade ground work was in progress. My job was now Adjutant, with the result that I spent most of my time getting to know our new intake and seeing that they were given good instruction. After they had become proficient at marching, squad drill, rifle exercise and extended order work I began to concentrate on their instruction in picqueting, camouflaging themselves and their sangars, withdrawals and attacks in the hills and musketry.

Many of the men who had been with us on the operations were promoted to NCO, and a few went up to Indian officer. It made my heart glad to know that they were now reaping the rewards of faithful and loyal service. They had proved themselves to be wonderful friends, besides being wonderful fighters.

Concentrated training continued for several months, until the new lads were considered fit to join the ranks and move into their sections under the new NCOs. The time sped for me, because in addition to doing the work of Adjutant I was also Second in Command. Stuck away in the unattractive fort of Murtaza, and the small bungalow alongside where we lived and had our Mess, besides work there was nothing else to do. With absolutely no amenities of any sort and miles away from wine, women and song, four or five of us British officers just turned our full attention to training the men.

Then the day came when Percy and I, with 400 Militia foot soldiers plus another fifty or so mounted infantry Militia, whom Barker had trained to the peak of efficiency, moved out of Murtaza post for the last time. We proceeded north across the *raghza* towards old Khirgi camp, passing on our way Girni fort, which I have mentioned before. Strong but isolated, it is named after a huge black mountain at the foot of which it is situated. This colossal burnt black rock, with awesome precipitous cliffs, rises many thousands of feet perpendicularly into the sky and it is the safe abode of the *markhor*, wild goat, the straight horn variety. Where they live no *shikari* can approach and, although I have questioned many locals on the subject of Girni Sar (mountain) and its *makhor*, I always had the same reply: 'There are hundreds of big horned *makhor* there, but they are quite inaccessible to the *shikari.*' Nobody has ever surmounted the peak or got anywhere near it. It is still probably the only one in the world which has never been conquered, and what intrepid mountaineer will risk a bullet or two as well as his neck to make the attempt? Like an enormous ogre, Girni Sar stands on the edge of the border halfway between Murtaza and Khirgi, as though a sentinel guarding that godforsaken land, a symbol of the fierce, black-hearted, tyrant people who through the years have never been subdued for long by any of the successive wars waged against them for the vile atrocities done by them to poor innocent villagers.

Swinging west at Khirgi camp, we proceeded up the Taki Zam route and arrived at Jandola camp where a large force had gathered, we being the last to arrive. After spending the night at Jandola the column marched not towards Palosina, but through a notorious and very narrow and precipitous gorge, the Shahur Tangi, due west of Jandola. At the west end entrance of this *tangi*, the Force encamped on a level bit of ground near where two streams meet. This camp, Split Toi, is situated in Mahsud country and a strong Militia fort that was built there later on blocked this very important route for Mahsuds. One of the two streams flows down east from south of Kotkai, and the other from Sarkai Obo, in the vicinity of which was the Mahsud village, the nearest one to Sarwekai.

Inclusive of Split Toi, the route had been secured for our move by other units in the area, but from there, moving up the Sarkai Obo stream, we carried out our own picqueting for protecting the column and its long trail of animals.

The system for picqueting now used was different to that carried out during the Jandola-Kotkai-Kaniguram operations. Then we put up impregnable, permanent-route picquets so that at any time, had the Force Commander desired, the column could have fallen back using their protection in the withdrawal. In this operation the column moved forward under temporary picqueting cover and as the rearguard came along it called in those temporary picquets. In other words, the force proceeded along in a moving protective box. As the picquets were called in they were sent up forward to be used again if necessary by the advance guard commander. The speed of the advance of the column was necessarily slow, being governed by the efficiency and speed of the picquets in taking a hill and afterwards withdrawing. Of course this system would not have been used unless the political situation was peaceful and there was little or no likelihood of strong enemy interference. In fact, the Political Department were trying out a new scheme combining the troops' own protective measures with Khassadar protection. The Khassadars were tribesmen specially engaged to protect routes and camps from their own hotheads. They were of course well paid (or bribed, if you wish to call it that) and only functioned in their own land, i.e. Mahsuds in Mahsud country and Wazirs in Wazirland. They carried their own arms and took up positions well outside the normal picqueting line that was invariably taken and held by our own troops. From afar they could persuade any of their malcontents to desist from attacks. They were clearly made to understand that their pay depended on the efficiency with which they kept their hotheads in check. Although this system was used, at no time were recognised Frontier warfare precautions slackened.

After Split Toi, our next camp was at Sarkai Obo, a Mahsud village near Sarwekai, and here an underground stream that is discernible in the Sarwekai gorge disappears under the dry nullah bed, and emerges in abundance, flowing steadily on past Sarkai above Split Toi. The Force encamped and had ample water for all the animals, a considerable number of which we had with us because of an anticipated longish stay in Wazir country. From our camp it was not possible to see the old Sarwekai fort as the Sarkai ridge was in the line of sight, but a day or two later when we advanced we were able to view the old post where I had spent so many of my days in the years 1917 to 1919.

Due to the shortage of water on the route beyond Sarwekai, and until the Wana Toi would be reached, the Force Commander decided to go straight through from Sarkai Obo to Wana itself. It was to be a long march, therefore we left very early in the morning and because the country was known to our Militia lads we took over all the picqueting duties with the aid of our mounted infantry. They came into their own once we got to the open country close to Madijan and beyond to Gurguri Narai. It was really great to watch a strong troop of the horsemen galloping in extended lines to the foot of a ridge, there quickly dismounting and leaving their horses to be held by a few men while the rest of them swarmed up and took their objective. Our men worked fast and it wasn't long before we crossed the path I had taken in the abandoning of Sarwekai and we passed the Sarwekai gorge to the basin covered in mazri palm, where I had shot black and grey partridge on many occasions. From here, looking over my right shoulder I could see the high walls of the old Sarwekai fort standing out grimly against the sky, with a huge gaping hole marking where the heavy gates had stood. These were now, most probably, guarding the entrance of some rich Mahsud's castle. What memories swept through my mind as we passed on. Many were of happy times but those of the last hectic hours before and during the evacuation of the fine old fort were harrowing and best forgotten – if possible.

After passing Gurguri Narai, the mounted infantry were withdrawn, as the hills beyond were too high for them to operate on safely. Soon we dropped into the Wana Toi valley and came to Karab Kot tower, which looked much the same as it did when I had last seen it; only the roof had been dismantled. The Khassadars had placed strong parties of their men to guard the right flank of the route at and beyond Karab Kot, where two high hills and a rock-strewn re-entrant were considered by the Political Agent, who was with the column, to be a likely danger point. The inhabitants of that area had expressed their hostility towards our re-entry and re-occupation of the Wana plain. To safeguard the column from our point of view, our Scouts in strength held the high ground on the left flank from where we looked down at fairly close range on the danger spot. Our arrival at the final objective was quite uneventful. No Wana Wazir was to be seen. They who had been foremost in behaving traitorously in the Wana crisis had fled into the hills and distant villages. Between Split Toi and Wana not a single shot had been fired at the column, and after our mounted infantry had encircled the post and galloped on beyond, our Militia men who moved into the deserted area. We were back in our old perimeter. A.R. Barker, Percy, myself and our South Waziristan Militia *jawans* had retaken our old headquarters.

The Force camped within the perimeter walls of old Wana and remained about four days, during which it moved out twice to show the flag. On one of these outings towards the very high mountain opposite Sisha Picquet and Karab Kot, which was known to harbour hostile elements, we were fired at going out as well as in the withdrawal. Our Scouts, as usual, were detailed as advance guard on the way out. And then as the Force just did an about-turn when close to the Inzar Narai to return to camp, our men were still in the unhappy position of being closest to the snipers and therefore having all the bullets directed at them. Although the range varied between six and eight hundred yards, and there was little chance of an aimed shot finding its mark because we moved well extended and did not stop, yet the fact that one is being considered a moving target, and that the sniper's rifle fires a bullet that can go through a human body at those ranges, was not exactly comforting. I and my *jawans* were glad when we got back out of range without a casualty. Personally I hated the thought of having one of my men needlessly killed or wounded. It was a silly operation which gained naught and left many of us angered.

A day or two before the main Force withdrew towards Jandola the news was broken to me that our 400 Scouts were to stay in Wana. With Percy, myself and our Scouts, a doctor, an engineer, a supplies officer and a British conductor to help the supplies officer were also to remain. It struck me as being strange that I, as commanding officer of this force, should not have been told beforehand that we would be going there to be the garrison (or semi-permanent garrison) of our previous Wana headquarters. Perhaps the political people had not made up their minds on this point – I can't say. I felt that 'the powers that be' were going to use our small garrison to induce the Wana Wazirs to come to some terms which they had not shown signs of accepting up to that time. These Wazirs had made a tremendous haul after the evacuation of the post in 1919: hundreds of rifles, hundreds of thousands of rounds of .303 ammunition, tons of rations, a quartermaster's store full of clothing, all the personal belongings of the men and the officers, and the wonderful and valuable collection of silver in the Officers' Mess. Clearly they were loath to part with this loot. When I used to think of it all I felt like going berserk. I had lost two of my most prized possessions: my double-barrel twelve-bore shotgun, which I had not taken to Sarwekai on my last trip, and also my little chestnut horse, which I had to leave behind me in Sarwekai.

When the main Force moved off on the return to Split Toi taking our mounted infantry with them, I couldn't help hoping that our small army left behind in the blue would never be called upon to evacuate the area, as had our Wana garrison three years previously when four of our eight British officers were killed and two others badly wounded, and many of our brave and loyal Militia men lost their lives. What an impossible operation they had been called upon to undertake. Now our first preoccupation was to make our defences secure. The perimeter of the camp was pulled in so that the smallest possible detachment could hold it against a fair-sized *lashkar*, in the event of some of the garrison being out on some other job. We had no worry regarding water. The old 'keep' was included in the new defence layout and it contained a good deep well that never went dry. Large reserves of rations and ammunition, also spare issues of clothing, were left behind for us to draw on. Besides this, convoys carrying replenishing rations came up under Khassadar escort every fortnight. Post was delivered daily, being brought up as before by donkey, switched along by a *badraga*.[5] I was very lucky in one respect: the political representative left to help me and manage the Khassadars (who were housed in the old political *sarai*[6] which our air force had tried to bomb and had missed) was none other than our previous Militia head clerk, who had since the evacuation transferred to political service. He was a grand little chap, a good friend of all of us and a man on whom I could rely absolutely. He had several well-paid agents, or spies, under him, so was always in a position to give me the very latest political information. This was most important and every day he reported the situation to me.

The British engineer officer who had stayed behind with us had been given full authority to build any defences I asked for, with the result that within a week or so we had our new perimeter ready with the old keep as a stronghold in one corner. The new defences were strongly wired and the old buildings of the previous area were flattened out. This latter operation brought to light and into my possession the only relic of our past Wana Officers' Mess. While the old armourer's shop was being flattened I happened to be there, and seeing something bright I picked it up. It was a pair of silver sugar tongs with SWM engraved on the top. These I kept for many years as a reminder of the old Wana days, until some servant stole this small article of sentimental value. Our Militia armourer was also a first-class silversmith and had most probably been given the tongs from which to make a replica.

To occupy our time, which soon began to hang heavily on our hands, we decided to build four long barrack rooms for the men and a few smaller ones for others. The cold months were ahead and the Indian officers were all for making the men as comfortable as possible. I approached the political folk through Ali Akbar, my friend, and they agreed to stand the cost of all the roofing material to be delivered at our site. This was good news, for we would not have been able to carry out our project without political help. It also helped to keep quiet the locals who had the contract to bring in the rafters and the matting material. This was brought in by them on camels from the west where the Marwetai Mountains were covered in pine forests. We divided our Force into four parties of about 100 each. Each party was given one barrack to construct, utilizing the clay and stones of the walls of the old post. The buildings of the four barracks was to be considered a competition and a time limit was set for completion, after which a committee would decide which of the four was the best built and the prize would be several fat sheep for a feast. Enthusiasm ran high, the competition was keen and the work was carried out in the best of spirits. Work could be done only during certain hours, for morning parades, physical training, squad drill, rifle exercise and musketry took up one and a half hours every morning, except on Saturdays and Sundays.

The barracks were finished well within the times fixed and the committee, composed of our Indian doctor, the garrison engineer, the supplies officer, the British conductor and Ali Akbar, walked round and inspected the buildings. The members found it most difficult to come to a decision and in the end, amidst shouts of approval from all, the size of the feast was enlarged so that everyone could enjoy the *palao*[7] that was to be cooked. All the Indian and British officers put their hands in their pockets to help pay for the lovely sheep and the rice and, of course, we were invited to the spread.

Once a week, instead of parade ground work a column would move out in one direction or another to carry out some small exercise on the Wana plain. We had been asked by the politicals to keep clear of villages and try to keep the peace. I was in full accord with this idea. We had not been told how long we would be on the plain and it was better to have peace (outwardly, at any rate) than open hostility, which would have meant restrictions on parade ground work, games of football and outings.

Only once during our sojourn on the plain were we fired upon by the Wana Wazirs. While on one of my weekly exercises with our lads, we had moved out, a column of about 250, westwards of the post and then wheeled south towards a long spur, Shin Warsak, round the foot of which flowed the Toi. Our advance party had arrived to within three or four hundred yards of the little stream when we saw a crowd of armed Wazirs rushing towards the spur which they swarmed up. We knew that they were up to no good, but didn't know what other Wazirs in the villages on the plain behind us would do. So to be on the safe side I despatched fifty men back to take up positions to ensure our safe withdrawal route. No sooner had my covering party rushed off than the tribesmen began to shoot down at us. Our *jawans* returned more than shot for shot and I don't think the Wazirs were enjoying being shot at, because their first few minutes of quite rapid fire soon turned desultory and eventually ceased. The heads of the tribesmen, which had been clearly visible against the blue sky as we looked up at them from the plain below, were therefore perfect marks to aim at and began to disappear from view. The firing stopped and I withdrew my men in short rushes, but we were not fired on again. This little affair demonstrated clearly the continued hostile attitude that the Wana Wazirs harboured against us and was a reminder for our men to keep vigilant when away from the security of the camp.

While we were in Wana a road had been completed through the dangerous and notorious Shahur Tangi between Jandola and Split Toi. News came through one day that strong gangs of Mahsud irreconcilables, after attacking and neutralizing the route picquets, had blocked in the pass from the front as well as from the rear, before attacking and completely looting a motor convoy that they had trapped. Most of the unarmed drivers and a British officer in one of the lorries had been slaughtered. Some Mahsud Khassadars were found to have been involved in this attack with the result that the whole tribe were again in bad odour with the British. However it stands to reason that the Mahsuds as a whole were jubilant at such an outstanding success.

Had the British Raj made an error of judgement? Our strong force in Kaniguram had failed to go right in amongst the Makin villages to impress upon them by force that, as they considered themselves to be the leaders of the tribe, the Maliks themselves would bear full responsibility and accept the dire consequences of any future misbehaviour on the part of any section of their tribe.

I never heard what the immediate outcome of the Shahur Tangi affair was but I have little doubt that the British remembered, because within a few years a camp was built on the Wana plain and was occupied by a strong force. In addition, not many miles from our old Kaniguram camp, a great standing, permanent camp was built on the Razmak plain. Six-inch howitzers, with their long range and enormous destructive power were kept there as a threat to the Mahsud chiefs. All their Makin villages and fine towers were within range of these big guns.

Nothing of any event took place in Wana in the months that followed. The Wazirs did not exhibit any outward hostility but were obviously disgruntled and showed it when we sometimes met. In fact, I had never noticed any friendliness in their attitude towards us. After the winter months our Wana garrison was withdrawn to Manzai, for the politicals had decided to try out yet another scheme, less dangerous than the one that involved keeping 400 Militia and a few British officers miles away. I was glad to get away and I am sure all the rest of the garrison felt as I did. Our camp was then taken over by Wazir Khassadars commanded by their own appointed headmen. Perhaps this sudden change of ideas by the Political Officer was precipitated by the Shahur Rangi disaster, for who knew what would happen next? Our small garrison away in Wana had been quite a tempting prize for the tribesmen to contemplate, and after every success by any of their gangs their tails went higher, their arrogance mounted and the obvious danger for a small isolated garrison increased.

Not long after the Shahur Tangi disaster and when we were back in Manzai, another nasty incident occurred which proved the absolute unreliability of these Wazirs. Little Ali Akbar, the political representative who had remained behind in Wana when we left, was on a tour to inspect the Khassadars of the line of communications. He sat quietly near the Madijan spring having his lunch when he was foully murdered by a bullet fired at him from close behind by one of the Khassadars. This was indeed tragic, for he had once been our Militia head clerk and was a general favourite with all of us, a really first-class chap, small to look at but with a big brave heart.

In Manzai we were well off. The camp had been greatly improved since we were last there and was now a military base. We occupied a very nice large bungalow with electric light and fans, while the men had comfortable barracks and, as well something they had not seen for months, charpoys to sleep on. A huge fleet of little Ford Vanettes brought up supplies for the army on the line of communications and to keep them in trim there was a modern workshop in the camp. For the protection of these daily Ford convoys a British armoured car unit patrolled the Manzai-Kaur Bridge ridge. It was good to see these fine Rolls-Royce armoured cars with swinging turrets and machine guns, manned by cheery British lads all itching for a scrap, which however they never had.

We had detachments in Khirgi camp and in a small post, Jatta, a little distance from Kaur Bridge, towards Murtaza. In Manzai we were responsible for the protection of the camp and in addition did road protection duties towards Khirgi. Life now was easy and enjoyable, and of worries there were none, nor of dangers. In fact the camp was considered safe enough for army nursing sisters to be sent there to look after the fine hospital that had been built. Competition amongst the officers to 'get off' with these nice lasses was keen, but unfortunately there was always the stern presence of a middle-aged matron in the offing, and to circumvent her was not easy. She looked after her little cluster more ardently than a mother hen does her chicks.

About this time I was asked if I would like to take on the job of SSO,[8] in addition to looking after our few hundred Militia lads in

119

Khirgi. Anything for a change from the rather monotonous life encouraged me to say 'Yes!' This, the very smallest type of staff appointment it was possible to hold in the army, which brought in a huge allowance of Rs30/– a month, took me, in work, about half an hour a day to get through. In a short while I had good reason to regret accepting the job. Manzai also had an SSO and I happened to have met him once or twice. As SSO I was issued with a set of pamphlets marked 'Most Secret'. These two or three little booklets had to do with sending and receiving secret messages in cipher. The SSO in Manzai also had a set of the same kind of pamphlets. One day he came across to Khirgi and asked me to lend him one of the little books, as he had a message to decipher but had mislaid the all important 'key', adding that he would return it to me the next day. I replied that I would be going to Manzai the next day and I would call in at his office to collect it. When I went along to see him the following day he denied that he had borrowed my copy of the secret booklet. Now I was in a stew, for every SSO had to sign a safe custody receipt for the complete set of pamphlets and also submit another such declaration monthly. I was now one secret document short. However, on my return to Khirgi I determined to report the matter to Brigade Headquarters, Jandola, where I knew the Brigade Major. So I rang him up and explained matters. He told me not to worry and that he would 'fix' things for my friend in Manzai.

A few days later, true to his word, the Brigade Major, on his return from Manzai, passing through Khirgi, handed me back my secret booklet. He knew the number of my set, which was printed on the cover of every pamphlet in the set. Every one has a different number and when he checked the Manzai set the stolen document was at once apparent. I was saved from a rap over the knuckles but the chap who had tried to do me down was sent back to his battalion with a flea in his ear. This was the only time in my service that a fellow officer let me down.

While in Khirgi one of my old Indian officers, a keen *shikari*, asked me to go with him to try and get a *chinkara*, which is a small deer, the male of which has straight horns. These timid and really beautiful slim beasts could be seen on most days on the *raghza* that came down from the low undulating hills just east of

Girni. They would feed at night on the sparse crops on our side of the border opposite Manzai, and would then wander back to their low hills at dawn. My *shikari* friend's idea was to take up positions on the halfway line early so as to be ready to intercept the deer on their way home. We had to have a good-sized guard with us, as the country is wild and more or less a no man's land. Leaving at about four in the morning we were in position an hour later. We camouflaged ourselves behind low sangars and dried-up bushes which grew in profusion in all of the shallow nullahs that went straight west to east, and then waited, keeping a sharp lookout. My friend and I were together and our men were spread out over an area of about 300 yards. If one man could not get a shot perhaps another would be luckier. I hadn't a rifle as I wasn't too keen on shooting one of the little animals. Sure enough, as the sun came over the horizon, a small herd of about five or six were seen coming leisurely, nibbling at plants as they advanced. Other groups of them could be made out far to the south. They would miss our line. There was only one male in the group that would pass by our hide. My friend was going to take a shot after the herd had passed on its way through so as not to endanger any other party of ours. They were quite unsuspecting as they passed and my subedar had his first shot at about 80 yards. He missed and in a flash the animals were away at terrific speed. They were really beautiful to watch, their bounding graceful in the extreme. High up in the air and at least 15 feet on was each bound. Their little backsides were white bulls-eyes and there couldn't be a marksman in the world who could hit one of those bobbing marks which, with each magnificent bound took it another five yards away. I wasn't sorry that my friend had failed to kill. We had had some fun and proceeded back to camp for breakfast. Our covering party was given a goat for their trouble, so they were pleased. They had *palao* for dinner that night and I was sent my share – after all, what is the difference between the flesh of a deer and that of a well-fed goat?

While our Militia were helping the Army in their duties they continued to issue us with free rations. Excellent rations they were. The British supply section saw that all British ranks got what was good for them and so we were in want of nothing. We had three or four outside officers attached to our Mess for feeding and so were a large and happy crowd. Every afternoon there was football, hockey or tennis to play and keep us fit, and after dinner we played bridge.

The months of May, June, July and August were hot, but the temperatures never approached the heat of the lower plain. The nights were often coolish, for Manzai is on a long, high ridge. At night we had our beds carried up to the roof of the Mess and so got any breeze that was going. When the heat stoked up badly we usually had a dust storm descend upon the small cantonment. Although these storms left all our belongings covered in a thick layer of red dust we could put up with this for the temperature always dropped by at least 10. Once, one of these storms brought such a blanket of red grit and dust that visibility was reduced to less than five yards. A short while later, with the hurricane, a rainstorm broke upon us and this rapidly developed into a fierce hail tempest of tremendous fury. For about an hour it hailed and hailed and hailed, not ordinary hail but huge stones the size of billiard balls. Even safe in our bungalow the intensity of the heavenly attack was quite frightening. Helped by the violence of the wind, the large hail struck the walls of the houses with the reports of rifle fire. The little Ford Vanettes parked on their parade ground in neat lines were swung round, turned upside down and had their glass windscreens smashed to pieces. Mules, camels and horses, driven half-crazy by the velocity of the hail, which left lumps on their backs and heads as big as a man's fist, raced about the camp trying to escape from the terrible bombardment. Some ran into the wire fencing that surrounded the cantonment, and in their frenzy cut themselves so badly on the barbs that they had to be destroyed later. Sheep and goats were killed outright, for their constitution could not bear up against the onslaught. Unfortunate people who lived in the double-fly EP tents had to flee for their lives, for it did not take long for the canvas to get riddled to let in the rain and hail. One poor chap tried to escape towards one of the bungalows, which became a refuge centre. He had emerged from his dilapidated tent without any headgear and was almost stunned before he had gone ten paces by three or four hail stones that gashed open his bald head. Returning to his tent and grabbing the large cover off his Remington typewriter, he ran to us with this over his head and so escaped further punishment. But he was in a bad way and had to be admitted to hospital for treatment. When the storm had exhausted itself it went on leaving Manzai in a white canopy of ice, and that night those of us who had blankets used them.

The months flew by and the autumn arrived. To amuse myself I had bought a motorcycle and sidecar. The machine was a solidly built BSA of about 4 or 5 horsepower. It had a belt drive and three-speed gearbox, so was quite capable of transporting two of us. I had bought it in 'Pindi[8] when on a few days' leave to hit the high spots of that large town. Once I got the engine going it was grand for touring. But to get the engine to fire I often had to push for 10 or 15 yards. The carburettor had a screw that lowered into the jet and, inexperienced in the ways of petrol-driven engines, I was never able to fully master the workings of that carburettor. Once the engine was warmed up I could start her with the kick-starter but on a cold morning pushing was the only solution. I loved that solid old BSA which, besides starting it up, never gave me any trouble and gave me and my friends many hours of enjoyment. Many times two of us would get aboard with shotguns (mine borrowed from a friend) and go off down the ridge after coveys of sisi or wild pigeon, which used to come in great flocks to feed on the horse manure that was, after removal from the camp lines, deposited a mile or two down the ridge. I remember on one occasion we spotted a large flock of pigeon settle behind a small mound, so the two of us crept up from behind the cover and in the resulting four shots bagged so many birds that the sidecar was filled. Not good sport, perhaps, but we had a change of diet in the Mess for a couple of days and so did several other messes, for we sent the spare birds round. Curried pigeon are lovely to eat.

As I mentioned earlier, our Militia had a detachment in a small post, Jatta, a few miles east of Murtaza on the main road which the garrison were responsible for protecting a couple of miles in either direction. Early one morning I was awakened by a telephone orderly for an urgent message from the Indian officer in command of Jatta. Dressing hurriedly I hastened to our office and spoke to the officer who was waiting for me at his end of the line. He told me that one of his men, while on sentry duty, had been wounded by a rifle shot that morning before dawn and would I please go down in an ambulance and take the man back to hospital as soon as possible, as he was in great pain. One ambulance was always kept on duty for urgent calls and, collecting a medical orderly, we piled in and went off down the ridge. We had no escort and were risking things. It was too early for the road protector troops and the four armoured cars to have been sent out. We arrived safely and went into the small room where the wounded lad, not more than eighteen, was sitting, nursing a horribly lacerated left hand. While the medical orderly was attending to the boy I went along to the place on the roof of the post where the sentry was said to have been found when the NCO of the guard, hearing the shot, went up to investigate. Sure enough, there was blood all over the place. The wall parapet was quite 4½ feet high and therefore it was most unlikely that the sentry's hand could have been struck by a bullet fired from outside the fort. The lad's rifle barrel was dirty, but no empty cartridge case was to be traced. Of course this could have been thrown away or hidden. Downstairs again the medical orderly, a Britisher, told me that the wound could not have been caused by a bullet fired from a distance. By this time I was quite satisfied in my mind that the poor lad, for some reason which I was never able to discover, had shot himself after placing the palm of his hand on the muzzle of his rifle and then pressing the trigger, probably using the big toe of his right foot. Back in Manzai and in the hospital, where a surgeon was ready to receive the case, we were told by him that the boy most probably would never be able to regain full use of the messed-up hand. He was right, the lad was discharged from the Corps and perhaps this is what he had been after. But what a dreadfully painful and crippling way to get his wish. By disabling himself he had committed a serious offence, however no action was taken against the lad, for heaven alone knows what the real reason was that caused him to do such a dreadful thing to himself. He himself refused to speak but one thing is certain, nobody would disable himself unless his mind was in a serious state of torment.

It was not many months later that we in the South Waziristan Militia received the shock of our lives: the Corps was to be disbanded forthwith. However, those of our men who wished to serve on to complete their service for pension could do so by transferring to the Mohmand Militia, a smaller corps than the South Waziristan Militia and located north of Peshawar and the Kabul River to guard the Indian frontier against incursions of tribesmen from the hilly Mohmand country to the west. Fort Shabkadar, the headquarters of this militia, was within an hour's run by car from Peshawar.

A large number of our men opted to serve on and I was asked to go in charge of them and look after their interests until they had settled into their new unit. I agreed. Except for our uniforms and bedding, which had been issued to us by the Army, everything else was handed in to the arsenal, so when we left Manzai we were an unarmed company of soldiers. Percy, my best friend and also my brother's, went to his active battalion, the Third Battalion of our 12th Field Force group, and to my sorrow I never met him again. Many of our Indian officers, staunch friends of mine, came along with me and helped me to look after our men on the journey to Shakadar. Most of them had a few more years to serve to qualify for their full pensions. I was not sorry to be leaving Manzai and looked forward to some social life which Peshawar would be sure to offer. But I made a miscalculation when I imagined that I had seen the last of the rough country I was leaving behind.

We were taken down to Tank by motorized transport and deposited at the small railway station. The railway transport officer had arranged accommodation all the way through to Peshawar and so we had no trouble on the way. At Peshawar we were met by lorries that took us along to our new headquarters, Shabdakar, a large fort which, besides holding 200 of our men, also had room for the officers' quarters and a comfortable Mess. On the top of a mound in the middle of the fort was a bungalow which had one enormous room and a bathroom, scantily furnished and obviously not having been occupied for ages. This was allotted to me, with the cheerful information that it was haunted. However I'm not in the slightest superstitious, so I moved in without hesitation. It turned out to be possibly the best set of rooms in that fort because being high up it got any breeze that was blowing, while the rooms below, surrounded by the high walls of the fort had the perpetual fug created by crowds of humans cooped up in a congested area. Although getting up meant the climb of a number of steps, I soon got used to this and liked my new dwellings. I was alone up there and had quite a good view of the surrounding country and bazaar that lay close to the fort.

Some years before a very famous Militia, the Khyber Rifles, had been disbanded when the Army took over all the Khyber fortresses and many of the men had transferred to the Mohmand Militia, as our men had now done. This corps differed considerably to all the others for an officer could visit by car all the posts, which were on good roads, within an hour or two and Michni, the nearest post to Peshawar, was only about half an hour's run on. Being so close to this fine large cantonment was naturally a great temptation for officers to rush down two or three times a week for tennis, parties and dances at the really first-class Peshawar Club. There were no restrictions regarding road-closure hours and therefore a party of officers could return in the early hours of the morning having been to a late dance for which the club was famous. Parades were left to the Indian officers to supervise, the office work was looked after by the Adjutant and Commanding Officer and the remainder of us officers toured up and down the road to the different posts, a peacetime militia if ever there was one. After years of Waziristan and its burnt-black rocks and fierce inhabitants I must admit I enjoyed the change of atmosphere and the fun and games of Peshawar. I had sold my BSA and left it behind in Manzai, and now invested in a new combination, a beautiful 6-horse power, twin-engine AJS. It had a large comfortable sidecar with wind-screen, luggage carrier and a spare wheel that could be changed with either of the cycle's wheels. I was as proud as Punch. In Waziristan there had been nothing on which to spend my pay so I was flush enough not to have to worry about money.

To protect the border from gangs sneaking across in the dark hours, thickly woven barbed-wire entanglements were erected between the posts, along the side of the roads nearest the border. For communication purposes between posts and also as lookout points, high towers were constructed inside some of the posts, but because of the peaceful conditions that had prevailed in the district during the last couple of years, most of these measures were falling into disuse and grass was growing within the wire strands, thus no steps being taken to keep the defences clear. It seemed to any discerning mind that the Mohmand Militia was fast becoming a superfluous unit. No money was being spent on the upkeep of the defences and the towers in the posts, with their high ladders leading to the top platforms, were becoming dangerous through lack of attention. One day, a few weeks before my joining the Mohmand Militia, one of the junior officers had scaled up to one of these platforms and on the way down, most probably due to the insecurity of the design of the contraption, fell to the ground, and when picked up was dead. Indeed a tragic and unnecessary death which had cast gloom not only over the Mohmand Militia, but also the Cantonment of Peshawar where the lad was well known and most popular.

After a few months in Shabkadar a surprise message was received in the office: the Mohmand Militia was to be disbanded forthwith and with this information came the news that a militia for South Waziristan was to be reformed, not with the name of South Waziristan Militia, but South Waziristan Scouts. This was good news to me and I was quite thrilled to know that, after all, my old militia was to be resuscitated.

Except for some men who preferred to leave rather than serve in Waziristan, and this included all but one of the British officers, the Corps was transferred lock, stock and barrel to Manzai. Naturally I accompanied the large party back again to my old haunts.

After sorting ourselves out, assisted by a new commanding officer and several newly appointed officers, the new South Waziristan Scouts settled down in Jandola, our headquarters. I was now the only old South Waziristan Militia officer still serving in militias, but to keep me company I still had a large number of old Indian officers and men, who were also glad to be back in the environment they understood. They had not been happy in Shabkada, not fitting in too well with the atmosphere existing there. Now it was different because they were back in their old corps – new name or old name. By recruitment the strength was increased to about 700 and before long, instead of holding the Gomal posts and Wana, we now took over Split Toi, the responsibility of the Shahur Tangi and up the Taki Zam to and inclusive of Sora Rogha.

The South Waziristan Scouts now had most of the office staff of the Mohmand Militia, who were a very efficient lot. For us officers we now had a complete Mess, a most comfortable one at that including much good silver, for what we had lost in Wana we inherited on the disbandment of the Mohmand Militia. A very large fort was being built on the Sora Rogha plateau and as it neared completion I was sent there with a few hundred men to garrison it. A British engineer officer was in charge of the construction and remained on with me for a short while to put in the finishing touches and add any extra details that struck me as being necessary. We got on well together and it was nice having another officer to share with me the first few weeks of my otherwise lonely stay in the fort.

Although the garrison of the new Sora Rogha fort was not as large as the one I had in Wana, yet I was happier now. Where before we had been in a dangerous situation, more or less isolated, we now had the Army behind us in close support when necessary and there was no likelihood of a few soldiers having to fight their way out of trouble on their own.

To open the road for convoys we picqueted down towards the Ahnai Tangi, where not many months before that great battle had been fought. Going there with a couple of hundred men was quite a frightening business, but never was a shot fired at us. What had happened to sober down the Mahsuds? It seemed that some sort of miracle had taken place in the last few months. Perhaps it was the building of this large and impregnable fort well inside their territory, which would always be a threat to their other habitations further afield. In addition there was the threat and declaration by the political authorities that the Wana and Razmak plains would be permanently occupied for breach of their agreements made at *jirgas*. At any rate, our route-picqueting proceeded week after week unmolested and, I may add, with hardly ever a Mahsud being seen. Our troops never relaxed precautions, for all the men knew what had happened not many months previously to the motor convoy in the Shahur Tangi. We were ever watchful for the slightest hint of trouble. The lessons that we had learnt while in the Waziristan Field Force we instilled into our new men and recruits. They were never to imagine that they were not being watched and plotted against by unseen Mahsuds.

After a few more months with the South Waziristan Scouts, and as general headquarters insisted that my time with militias had to come to an end, I was recalled to Jandola from Sora Rogha. I bade farewell to my old warriors who gave me a happy send-off from the past and for the last time when in militias, I proceeded down the valley of the Taki Zam, past the old battlefields where so many Indian soldiers had lost their lives in the year 1920.

I stayed in Jandola a short while and handed over my jobs of Second in Command and right wing commander to an officer who had been with my brother and myself in the Cadet College, Quetta in 1916, and who had just transferred to militias.

My last night, leading well into the day of my departure, was eventful. I'd had my last meal in the Mess and as I was leaving early I had said my goodbyes and gone to bed. A few hours later I was rudely awakened by the sound of rifle fire. Getting out of bed I pulled on my shorts and shirt, slipped on my *chaplies* and went out into the darkness. My orderly, knowing my habits, was at the door of my tent and told me that our men had taken up alarm posts but that the firing was from the camp adjoining ours, that was occupied by two companies of a regular Indian Army battalion, the remainder of the battalion being in the fort along-side the camp. Taking a few men I went along to the next camp to find out what was wrong, for some firing was still going on from their perimeter picquets. I was told that a British officer and three or four men had been shot by someone or other. As I could find no officer of the battalion I went to the fort and persuaded the guard to let me in. There I met a British officer who told me that the situation was still obscure but that an officer and three men had been shot and were in the hospital in the fort. In the operating theatre a couple of doctors were attending to the wounded. The wounded British officer, a great friend of mine and Second in Command of that battalion, was lying on a stretcher, gasping his last and beyond all medical help. He was quite unconscious and died quietly while I was there. By the time I was out of the hospital the firing had ceased and I was able to find out the details of the tragic incident. Apparently my friend had been going round the guards to inspect them, when one of his men, who harboured a grudge on account of some promotion question, shot him two or three time and then, running amok shot others who approached until a NCO put a bullet into him. Some of the men in the camp picquets became jumpy and commenced to fire into the night, imagining that the camp was being attacked. On the whole a very sad and regrettable affair.

I went back to bed at 3.00 a.m. but not to sleep. Sad and shocked at what I had witnessed I lay awake pondering on the unusual happenings in life, the sudden death of a fine officer and good friend, taken when in the seemingly perfect security of his surroundings for some unaccountable reason, and that this shocking drama should take place only a few hours before my long tour with militias in Waziristan terminated.

By 6.00 a.m. my servant and I, with our kit, were on our way in a 30 cwt lorry through Khirgi and Manzai, and on to Tank. Here I unloaded at the officers' rest camp, had a late breakfast and then tried to make up for some of the loss of sleep the previous night. That evening, catching a goods train on the miniature line I stretched out on my camp bed which my servant put up for me in a goods wagon that was going down empty. We arrived at Kalabagh at about 5.00 in the morning and removed my stuff to the little refreshment room that I knew so well. I spent the day there, for it was pleasantly cool by the river and I did not wish to travel again until night. I preferred to sit that day by the lapping waters of the Indus and think back on what I had left behind: militiamen, Pathan friends I could never forget.

My active battalion, the 2nd Battalion of Queen Victoria's Own Corps of Guides, Frontier Forces, had been transformed into the training battalion of the 12th Frontier Force of the Regiment, and so my active battalion was now the 1st, known to all as the Guides. The Commanding Officer, knowing the long period I'd put in with militias in Waziristan, and as the Guides were preparing to go on a tour of two years to Aden, arranged for me to get a nice soft job: Assistant Recruiting Officer, Pathans. This meant that I would be stationed in the most delightful little cantonment of Abbottabad, tucked away amongst beautiful hills north-west of Rawalpindi and on the border of Kashmir. I was indeed in luck's way for no nicer, prettier or happier station is there in the whole of India. As my job entailed a great deal of serious touring, collecting recruits for training for the active battalions that took Pathans, I had to buy a car. My touring took me south from the district of Kohat, where Khattaks and Bangash live, to far up north in the Black Mountain[10] district close to Abbottabad, where I collected Tanaolies, also down the Indus below Attock from where cis-Indus Khattaks come.

During my tours I met several old South Waziristan Militia pensioners in their villages as well as several men on leave. These old friends could never do enough to make me welcome in their small homes and what a pleasure it was to meet them.

Abbottabad itself is one of the most friendly stations I've ever been in. Everyone knew everybody and there were no cliques, with the result that the little club, a jolly rendezvous for all, arranged most of the fun and games: tennis tournaments, swimming galas, cricket matches and weekly dances. As the shopping facilities were limited because the cantonment was fairly small, people would motor into 'Pindi for a day's spree of buying, returning the same evening in time for dinner.

My year's tour of Assistant Recruiting Officer, Pathans, was all too short and I was very sorry to leave, but one year was as long as an officer was permitted to do as ARO. The Guides were now in Aden and as I had not had any long home leave in my ten years' service, I applied for some – to my surprise I was granted a full year's furlough in Blighty.

Leaving my car, a 10-hp Fiat with friends with whom I had shared a bungalow, I packed and headed for Bombay that was the port from which the weekly P&O mail steamers sailed. I had booked a passage on the *Narkunda* and had a wonderful voyage, except for a day or two when we sailed through 'The Bay', which kept up her stormy reputation.

I found a year too long a time in which to do nothing important and only spend money, which after eight months had drained dry, so I cut short my furlough and sailed to join my battalion in Aden. My advice to anyone who has never been there and has a hankering to go is 'don't'. It's a dreadful spot to be stationed in and the British eventually gave up the port.

The barracks for the men and the officers' quarters and Mess were in the Crater, a mile or two inland from the port. Situated in the extinct mouth of an ancient volcano, with horrible dry lava hills surrounding the area, everyone who was unfortunate enough to be housed there was deprived of not only the one redeeming feature of the port, a view of the sea, but also any cool breeze that happened to be blowing.

A company of the Battalion was on detachment duty on an island some distance towards the Red Sea. This island of Perim was a coaling station and the officer who commanded the detachment (and I think also the island itself) was welcomed by the well-to-do coal authorities only if he was capable of putting down, without heat taps, several glasses of whatever beverage was being consumed at the time, but of course alcoholic. The island was quite a popular place to go to for a month or so, for there was good fishing and sailing to be enjoyed besides the drinking parties. In Aden everyone went to view the 'mermaid' once. As far as I can remember, on the Aden seafront the charge was about a rupee to be allowed into the small room where the stuffed atrocity was kept in a glass case. Had the charge been one anna it would have been excessive. One thing can be said about mermaids in general: if they are all like the one I saw no self-respecting sea god would be seen dead with one.

[Editor's note: Cumming was privileged to have served with two of the most rough-and-ready, indeed legendary corps raised on the Frontier, the Corps of Guides and the South Waziristan Scouts. To Sir Henry Lawrence, British Resident at Lahore, who was later to die a hero at the Siege of Lucknow during the Mutiny, the Corps of Guides owes their name and origin. In 1846, a few months before the Sepoy Mutiny, Lawrence gave Lieutenant Harry (later Sir Harry) Lumsden the task of raising a corps of native irregulars to gather intelligence on tribal movements and act as guides to the troops in the field. In the twenty years between the end of the Mutiny and the start of the Second Afghan War in 1878, the Guides fought heroically in almost every expedition that was sent out against their Pathan kinsmen. The Corps of Guides was merged with the 1st Punjab Cavalry in 1849, when it became known as the Punjab Irregular Force, or 'Piffers'. The modern incarnation of the Guides is known as the Frontier Force Regiment, the result of an amalgamation in 1957 of the Guides, the Frontier Force Regiment and the Pathan Regiment. Cumming joined the 2nd Battalion Guides in Malakand and wore, as he mentions, a 'khaki serge jacket'. The Guides were the first army unit to adopt this style of dress that blended in with the landscape. In doing so, they set a precedent in military history by outfitting their men in tunics and puttees of this new colour called 'khaki', an Urdu word of Persian origin meaning 'dusty' or 'dust coloured'. Lawrence, in conceiving this unconventional force, appears to have taken his inspiration from Napoleon's elite Guides. Sir Harry Lumsden was the Guides' first commanding officer and its only British officer. The Corps was formed of one troop of native cavalry and two companies of infantry, about 300 men in all. The commander had no trouble finding recruits, who were for the most part drawn from the Pathan tribes. Aside from the excitement of soldiering on the Frontier, the Guides received a higher rate of pay than sepoys of the Regular Army. The Guides' unorthodox and homely appearance quickly earned them the nickname of 'Mudlarks', although it is safe to assume that many a sepoy would have secretly wished for similar clothing to render them less obvious targets for Pathan bullets. In fact, it is surprising that the Army had not acknowledged earlier the need for some suitable bush uniform. Certainly the British soldiers who faced American militiamen in the War of Independence, as well as the War of 1812, would have benefited from some type of camouflage. Their red uniforms stood out like beacons for the enemy, who were for the most part clad in homespun garments that blended with the forests and hills.

In the twenty years between the end of the Mutiny and the start of the Second Afghan War in 1878, the Guides fought valiantly in almost every expedition that was sent out against their Pathan brethren.]

Chapter 5

Out of Waziristan, Into the Fire

When I joined the Guides in Aden the Battalion had nearly completed the two-year tour, and after a month or two we all sailed to Bombay in a troop ship. Everybody in the Battalion was overjoyed for we were returning to our own peacetime station, the small but pretty town of Mardan, which had been the home town of the Corps of Guides, the infantry and the cavalry regiment of the same name ever since it was raised by the famous old soldier, Harry Lumsden, before the Indian Mutiny.

A troop train was ready to receive us at Ballard pier, Bombay, and it did not take many hours for our seven hundred men to unload from the steamer and load all our kits and baggage into the train.

Not many months after returning to Mardan I was detailed by the General Officer Commanding Peshawar Division to carry out propaganda tours amongst the Yusafzais, Pathans who come from the Mardan area. My only qualifications for this which, after all was a civilian's job, were that I knew Pashtu and the Pathan fairly well. As regards the propaganda side of the new job, I didn't even know where to start. However, I made friends with the Assistant Commissioner and the Assistant Superintendent of Police; with their help my tour programme was made out and I was given a general idea of what to talk about. During those times an anti-government movement was being organized by local agitators who called themselves 'Khudai Khitmatgaran',[1] in other words the Servants of the Almighty. These locals, most probably under

134

the payment of other anti-government organizations in India, wore dark red clothing and everyone, including the press, referred to them as 'Red Shirts'.

In fact some of them considered themselves so red that they paraded about in gangs with their hands and faces daubed with red paint. The police, also Pathans, were continually clashing with these bands of agitators who were disrupting the normal and peaceful life of the District, bricks often began to fly and lathis[2] were often used as a result. In one encounter an enraged police-man who had been hit by a stone thrown by a completely red-painted Red Shirt, shouted aloud for his own friends as well as the other side to hear, 'Come, let's pull down his *partoogai* and see if he has painted his arse red as well.' And when a movement was made in the direction of accomplishing what had been suggested by this jibe, an uproar was created, for the Pathans are averse to being seen naked below the navel. Moreover, the insulted man was none other than the leader of the Red Shirts in Mardan, judging from the many pips, crowns and crossed swords with which he had adorned his shoulder straps.

On these tours I was always accompanied by the Assistant Superintendent of Police with whom I became firm friends, and with his beautiful twin sister as well. We never went into the countryside without an armed escort of police, for a job some-times led us into perilous situations, especially when near the Yusafzai-Gowdon border where villagers had arms, unlicensed and difficult to check.

On one occasion Jack and I were proceeding side by side along a narrow way through a village when an old woman cast a huge stone down towards us from a housetop. Thank God it landed between us and not on one of us, for it was weighty enough to have cracked a skull. At the time I could not help recalling to mind the Bible story of Abimelech and the woman of the tower of Thebez, who cracked his skull by throwing an upper mill stone on to him.

On another occasion we visited a large village near the border and because of its situation and the large number of instigators who were known to be in the vicinity, the Assistant Commissioner had insisted on a squadron of cavalry going along in case of trouble. It was as well that we had a strong escort for we hadn't been long in the village before a crowd commenced to gather and surround Jack, myself and our posse of police as we were talking to the friendly elements whom the *malik* of the village had collected for us to lecture. After shouting a few slogans the unruly ones began to show hostility not only towards our party, but also towards our villager friends. As this looked like increasing and the accumulating crowd outnumbered us by about twenty to one as they began to press towards our small circle, I hurriedly scribbled a note to the Major who was commanding the cavalry squadron, asking him to close in on the village and show that they were there to protect us from violence. When we had approached the village the cavalry had remained about 300 yards back and out of sight, so the villagers probably were unaware that they were there. I had warned the commander that I would call for help if necessary. The policeman I gave my note to was able to get through without raising any suspicion and in about ten minutes the Squadron had closed in on the village and surrounded it by section groups. The angry throng had not noticed the cavalry moving in. They continued to shove and push towards us and the situation became tense. When the officer commanding the Squadron came trotting along with a dozen or so tough-looking horsemen carrying lances, their threatening attitude dissolved as rapidly as butter does in a hot pan. We had had a nasty moment or two and there is no doubt that the cavalry arrived opportunely. I have been in a few bad situations at different times but this was undoubtedly the most frightening of all. In cold blood the lot of us could have been murdered. Jack and I were grateful to the cavalry for their timely assistance.

Shortly after the above incident we were bound for a village where the pensioners and men on leave from the Army were being coerced by the large number of Red Shirts in the vicinity. Some of the staunch old Indian officer pensioners called for help and support to combat the inroads that the semi-aggressive tactics of the agitators were making. Our aim was to encourage and persuade the younger generation to resist the overtures of the Reds. As this village was within a mile of the one where we had trouble previously I took along an escort of about fifty men from the Guides and the Assistant Commissioner had made arrangements

for a magistrate to accompany our party to hand over responsibility to the Army in case the situation turned serious. Were a
riot to develop from one of these Red Shirt confrontations with
the Armed Forces, Jack and I were determined to be in a position
of strength and not again to be caught in the terrifying situation
we had experienced the previous week. This time the Red Shirts
had assembled from several directions, congregating at a point on
our approach track. It was clear that they were out to prevent us
getting to our village. On the other hand, we had to get there. To
turn back because a few hundred agitators were trying to block
our way was unthinkable and would have resulted in increased
unlawful acts as well as loss of 'face'.

Jack knew the law and understood his job thoroughly. He had
his police in front as we walked towards our objective and my
men followed a hundred yards behind. From a distance the mass
of red-coated villagers marched towards us. The magistrate went
on ahead to ask them what they wanted and in reply they shouted
their slogans and waved their lathis in emphasis. They continued
to advance along the track, blocking it completely. By assuming a
hostile attitude, clearly backed by their huge numbers, they were
out to deter us from going on. The confrontation began to get
threatening and, when they refused to listen to reason and their
advance towards us became dangerously close, the troops were
called forward and formed a double line in front of us. Only
about 10 or 15 yards separated our party from the angry mob,
now frustrated in their attempt to scare us off the track. The
magistrate, realizing that the situation was worsening and getting
beyond civil control, handed me the written authority to use whatever force was necessary. 'Fix bayonets, on guard!' was the first
order, and with a rattle of metal on metal the fifty bayonets were
now pointing at the mob. This did not deter them and abuse
and stones were flung at us as they came closer, pressed on from
behind by their more protected and therefore less likely to be
frightened companions. The next order, 'Load', was given – now
when the Red Shirts saw and heard the live rounds snap into the
breeches of the rifles they began to waver. They did not wait for
the next order, which would have been 'Aim', given to two or
three selected NCOs. Their front line broke and these men darted
back, mingling with the crowd, their second line, now exposed,

also turned and fled, and in a minute the way for us was clear. The troops unloaded, the police moved up again to the front, I returned my order to the magistrate and so we were able to proceed on to complete our work.

A few more weeks of touring and the propaganda job ended, for I was attached for duty to the group's Territorial Battalion that every year was embodied for a couple of months for training. I submitted my tour report to the General Officer Commanding and received a letter of appreciation in return, so I considered my sweat, risks and trouble well rewarded. I had been lucky in having a good friend in the Assistant Superintendent of Police with whom to tour, and on our return from a long walk in the country, we found his charming sister Jill waiting for us with a scrumptious tea.

With the Territorial Battalion in Nowshera, 15 miles east of Mardan, it was easy for me to go into my headquarters when off duty when any tennis or polo tournament was being played there. Not that I played polo. I was never able to afford to keep more than one pony, and to take up polo seriously, a minimum of three ponies is necessary. Many of our Guides' cavalry officers kept four and five of their own, besides having the choice of others out of the Squadron they happened to be with. Every officer in the cavalry was expected to play, consequently only those who had private incomes or substantial allowances from their people were able to go into a cavalry regiment. But whether one played or not, there is no game more worthwhile watching than a good game of polo, and the polo in Mardan was always good when a tournament was on, for the best teams of the Division used to come along to play on our two beautiful grounds.

Only Pathans were taken into the Territorial Battalion of our group and it was because of this and my knowledge of the language that I was attached to the unit for their training period. It was good fun, and I enjoyed being in Nowshera and meeting lots of new people in their two months' training. The keen soldiers learnt not only to march, do squad drill, company drill and rifle exercises, but also to use their rifles with efficiency. Of course this last comes naturally to a Pathan.

   Back with the Battalion I was put in command of B Company, which had a couple of platoons of Pathans, one of Sikhs and one of Dogras, and I also took charge of the Machine-Gun Company. These two companies remained in my charge and my responsibility throughout my service with the battalion.

Several weeks after returning to Mardan I was sent off on a refresher machine-gun course to Ahmednagar. Travelling down by the Bombay Mail which I caught at Nowshera, I found that my reserved bunk had been booked in a two-berth coupé which I had to myself. Next to my compartment was another coupé occupied by two officers, friends both bound for the same course as myself. All that day and throughout the following night we rattled along at a good speed, nobody came in to share my coupé and I had turned in to sleep at about ten. Always an early waker, I was up at dawn as usual, longing for a cup of tea and some hot toast. The train had come to a stop at a station and, unbolting the window and letting it down, I stuck my head out to see if my bearer happened to be about. Instead of seeing my servant a ghastly sight met my gaze: a crowd was gathered at the door of the next compartment and first one blood-covered figure was deposited on to a stretcher and then a second on another. These were then carried past my coupé and I recognized the faces of the two young officers who had occupied the next-door compartment. I dressed hurriedly and followed after where the stretchers had disappeared through the main porch of the railway station. I made inquiries and found that a railway hospital was just across the road and that the two officers had been taken inside. Going in I found a doctor attending to one, who was in a dreadful condition with knife stabs in the chest and abdomen. The doctor tried his best but the lad died after a minute or two. While he was being attended to I spoke to the other officer, who was also wounded but not too badly. He told me that he had been awaked by the screams for help from his friend who was on the lower bunk, while he was on the upper. In the dim light he saw two naked black figures attacking his companion with knives and had jumped down on top of one of them, knocking him down and snatching the knife from his hand. He then attacked the second assassin who had come to his friend's aid and in the fight he had been struck a few times. Both men then grabbed open the door and jumped out. He had fainted from pain and loss of blood, only regaining consciousness when the train was halted at this station and someone, seeing the blood flowing out from under the door, had opened it. This young officer had not been dangerously hurt and I heard later that he recovered completely and returned to his battalion.

As the train was whistling to move off I had to wish the wounded officer a hurried farewell and run to get into my compartment. This case didn't end there and had a sequel. In snatching the knife from the man onto whom the officer had jumped he had cut off the top of one of the man's fingers, which was later found on the floor of the coupé. When that assassin went for treatment to a village hospital he was apprehended and this led to the arrest of his companion. Both men were hanged.

When I had attended a machine-gun course in early 1917 it was to learn about the old Maxim machine guns of which each battalion had been issued with one section (two guns). They were reliable and accurate but their colossal weight went against them. To manhandle in hilly country they posed a big problem. The new Vickers machine guns that were issued to units were wonderful weapons: light, accurate and absolutely reliable. They were, moreover, easily moved about in the hills and in my opinion, in Frontier warfare, were unapproachable with regard to efficiency in giving immediate, close and accurate sustained fire in covering an attack or a withdrawal. I speak from personal experience for on many occasions, when in Razmak in 1935 to 1937, our battalion machine guns proved their worth.

A year or two later our battalion was detailed for a two-year tour of duty in the Khyber Pass. A brigade of infantry was always in position guarding this famous gateway into India and from Landi Kotal, a small cantonment where we first went, the Afghan border is just across the way. The four infantry battalions of the Brigade took it in turns to occupy the forts in the pass or remain in the comfortable cantonment. As a good road as well as a broad-gauge railway ran up the pass almost alongside each other, it was quite easy to get down to Peshawar for a weekend spree and, of course, officers took it in turn to get away. In the Peshawar Club there were several small bachelor cubicles where one could park oneself for a weekend and get food from the club dining room.

Landi Kotal had its own small club and members could play tennis, bridge or look at the latest illustrated London papers. For the men there was always hockey and football, rifle shooting and revolver matches. Also, a proportion of the men were permitted to visit Peshawar on short leave. As a training ground for platoons, companies and battalions, Landi Kotal had few equals, and the surrounding terrain gave scope for open, modern as well as mountain warfare. Although not a family station it was peaceful enough for parties of visitors, women and men, to come up, view the famous pass and have lunch in one of the officers' messes before returning to Peshawar.

After a few months in Landi Kotal the Battalion moved halfway down the pass to occupy the forts that protected the railway and the road. Shagai, a huge, pink-looking, brick-built fort held the headquarters and most of the Battalion. This fort I found most comfortable. The men had spacious barracks, the officers' quarters and Mess were really first class and in the middle of the large fort there was a long narrow swimming pool that gave great delight to all on a hot day. Unfortunately, most of the time that the Battalion was in Shagai my company was detailed to man the forts of Ali Masjid.

Perched high up on a precipitous crag that rose up in the centre of the narrow gorge, only one narrow rocky path led up from the valley stream to the two grim, grey stone little fortresses. One of these contained quarters for the unlucky officer stuck up in this inhospitable, hurricane-swept, prison-like place. A week up there was enough to drive one potty. However, my men were with me and what I had to put up with they had to – I expect they hated the fort as much as I did. There was no space large enough to do section drill, let alone platoon or company drill. I kept the men fit by making those not on guard duty run down to the bottom and back again every morning. To keep up our smartness we had to be content with rifle exercises and guard-mounting drill.

The nights were hideous. Regularly as clockwork, the wind would rise to tempestuous violence and roar through the tunnel-like defile and crags, seemingly even trying to sweep the two forts away. In days gone by some nervous-minded officer had made his men tie to the strands of the barbed wire defences empty tins, in many of which reposed small stones. That officer's idea was that on a still night a rifle thief or other *badmash* trying to get into the defences would give himself away.

I had sent for fishing tackle to amuse myself in the afternoons and went up or down the stream looking for the odd pool where snow trout lurked. They were small but delicious eating. My Punjabi-Mohammedan bearer who had been with me in Waziristan knew how to cook them to my liking. Sometimes a few of my men would accompany me to the stream. Their idea of fishing was to divert the stream above a likely area until the water, flowing away, would leave the fish high and dry and easy to collect. Gurkha troops were absolutely adept at this sort of game and I'm sure my men had learnt it from them.

No senior officer ever came to inspect our company forts. The climb up to the summit where we were perched involved really strenuous going, so I can't really blame anyone for avoiding a call on Ali Masjid. Once a week I went down to Shagai for a walk and to bring back a few library books and the weekly illustrated papers the mess had finished with. But what the Company missed most in this segregated spot was not being able to play a game of football or hockey. Years ago in the Afghan War,[3] towards the end of the last century, a great battle had been fought at Ali Masjid and the heights had been taken by our troops. A bar to a Frontier medal had been given for that fight, but after being there for a month I wondered whether it had been worth the bloodshed.

The Battalion's two-year tour in the Khyber came to an end after another six months in Landi Kotal, which helped to remove from me the horrible effects of a month or more in Ali Masjid. We returned to Mardan and many friends were there to greet us. Our lovely Mess garden was looking its best in early spring and once we had settled into our bungalows, Mardan and the Guides gave an at-home for all who wished to come. Late into the evening, with magic lanterns hanging from the many branches and our band playing soft music, the garden looked and felt like fairyland, and the air was laden with the scent of flowers. Our mess servants flittered round with trays of drinks, sandwiches, cakes and snacks of many kinds. Besides being a homecoming, that year was also an anniversary for the Guides cavalry and infantry. The officers did not spare themselves in any way to make the huge party a success. Many of the guests had been invited to stay on late and after supper we all danced on the lawn, on which had been stretched an extra large-sized tarpaulin, smothered by tins and tins of French chalk to make the surface really nice.

Later that year my turn for furlough came round again and I was in England for seven months touring round the south coast in a second-hand Austin that I bought for a song. The firm I bought it from were true to their word, for although the old two-seater was sound as a bell and never let me down once before returning to India, I sold the car back getting almost as much as I had paid for it. I journeyed across France by train and before catching my P&O ship at Marseilles, I spent a week in Switzerland, that clean and enchanting little country.

On rejoining the Battalion I was posted to the training unit, which had moved to Sialkot in the Punjab a few years previously. Again I met my brother who was doing a second tour with the training unit of our group. It was good fun being together and we spent our hot-weather leave in Srinagar, in Kashmir, on the Dal Lake, living in a houseboat, motoring about the beautiful countryside, picnicking in the wonderful old Mogul gardens or just lazing on the deck of one of the bathing boats anchored in the middle of the lake. If one got fed up with lake life there was the Club with its polo, tennis and dancing until all hours. Lots of people go to Kashmir for the good golf that can be had in the little hill health resort of Gulmerg. Here the setting for the links is grand and after a round or two there is, again, the Club, where everyone in Gulmerg congregates for beer and sandwiches. If on the other hand you are after romance, well, what could be more romantic than hiring a *shikara* with a good crew, collecting the girl of the moment and then, with a full moon to help, sliding over the calm waters of the Dal for just as long as you like, if your girl will allow you.

We had a wonderful holiday together and then motored back to Sialkot and our training of recruits. Life in the Training Battalion was a busy one, for besides drill periods three times a day, school work had to be supervised, games had to be encouraged as well as athletics, and on top of all this there was always office work and Commanding Officers' reports.

I was not destined to complete my two years' tour with the Training Battalion because of a short but ferocious war with Mohmand tribesmen across the border west of Shabkadar. The Guides Infantry was included in the small force that engaged the enemy in battle, suffering heavy casualties in men and officers. Only four British officers had been with the Battalion in the engagement and all four were casualties: two killed and two wounded. Within a few hours of receiving this sad and disturbing news, another officer from our 4th Battalion and myself, with about 150 men as reinforcements, entrained for the front. At Peshawar our party detrained and we had a wait of a few hours while motorized transport was collected to take us across the Mohmand border and on for a few miles to Lakai, where the small force was encamped.

I called in at the Indian military hospital to visit our wounded *jawans*, some of whom were my own B Company lads. Already some of the mothers and other family members had arrived from their villages to see their loved ones. These village folk were fortunate for their soldier sons or relatives would live. But there were many homes in the distant villages into which sorrow had swooped with frightening suddenness, because of a message delivered by the telegraph peon or the village postman, 'Regret the death in action of ...'

In England, 7,000 miles away, two families were plunged into grief, each having received the same kind of message that had been delivered at the homes of the bereaved ones in Kangra, Amristar, Kohat or Mardan districts. And in our battalion home town, Mardan, there was also grave sorrow and burning tears could not be held back, nor the accompanying sobs in sympathy. Jill, my friend Jack's sister, was now a young widow. Only recently married and expecting her baby, she had been wed to our Adjutant while I was in the Training Battalion in Sialkot. What a tragedy, married and bereaved, both within a short year. In a few weeks the young widow was to sail for England, there to receive from our King a small bronze cross inscribed with the words 'For

Valour'. A fitting decoration for a very brave young officer, posthumously awarded.

Because of our British officer casualties I remained on with my active battalion after these short Mohmand operations in which, since my arrival with the reinforcements, nothing more in the way of fighting took place. I marched the Battalion back to Mardan in three stages and there handed over to an officer who was senior to me and who had been left behind to look after the depot. More of our officers were recalled from outside jobs to which they had been seconded. Two new subalterns arrived from Sandhurst and we were up to strength in officers again. After the battle, Geoff Hamilton, recovering from his wound, rejoined to serve again in the Guides. He was awarded the Distinguished Service Order for his outstanding gallantry in that action and was one of the youngest officers in the Indian Army to gain this high award.

A year later the Battalion moved to the vast plain south-west of Peshawar. Here two battalions were stationed to guard Peshawar and its vital water supply from any further tribal invasion, as had taken place in 1919–1920. Our battalion occupied Fort Salop and a smaller company post, Jhansi, while the other battalion occupied the fort of Bara, situated on the water supply itself that was diverted from the Bara River a little distance further west. The river flows down from the Afridi mountains from which hordes of tribesmen swarmed down in the troubled years I have earlier mentioned, to make life difficult for all in the district, even in the huge cantonment of Peshawar itself.

I was lucky to be sent with my company and also the Machine-Gun Company to Jhansi post on the river. The hutted camp was really comfortable for all ranks and as there was a *maidan* outside the post, we soon converted part of it into hockey and football grounds. A strange point about this plain was that it bred hundreds of large scorpions. These were not seen during the daytime but at night they would come out of their holes. I did not realize that there were large numbers of these horrible poisonous creatures until one day, when we were practising live grenade firing, we saw a number of them in each small crater which the exploding grenade made. We now knew that they lived not far below the surface of the ground. We were lucky to have had only three or

145

four men stung, all at night. Only once during my six months at this post were we fired at and that was very mild shooting that did not hit anyone. I was carrying out a combined company/machine-gun scheme, a withdrawal, when some *badmash* fired at us from a distance.

Our next move was to the well-known and famous Fort Jamrud at the exit of the Khyber Pass. This huge fortress was well able to house the whole battalion but we had a few men out in smaller posts. Peshawar, now only a few miles away, was an attraction for us officers as it had been before for the Khyber Rifles' militia officers. Married officers stationed in Bara, Jamrud and the Khyber were allotted rooms in mansions specially built for their families, with the result that at most weekends only the minimum number of officers remained in the posts. As times were peaceful there was no harm in this.

In the Guides, after every three years in the Battalion, an officer's turn came round for home leave: eight months in England with his passage paid by the Government. My turn came round while I was in Jamrud and I went off to enjoy a long holiday.

I rejoined in Mardan, for the Battalion had returned before my leave expired, and for the next two years we were left in peace to enjoy our little home town. During this period I was invited by the Wali of Swat (the ruler of a small kingdom west of the Malakand) to a duck shoot a few miles inside his territory. Here many acres of rice were under water and hundreds of duck – mallard, pintail, teal and pochard – came to feed. The Wali, a very fine shot with a scatter-gun, had built four or five butts in the area of the shooting ground. After spending the night in his shooting lodge and being fed by his retainers with many delicious Pathan dishes, we all moved out early, before dawn, to take up our places. A couple of men to collect the birds went along with each gun and piloted him to his hide. I was very fortunate in that I had been lucky enough to draw the best butt. Going along quietly in the dim light I could hear the quacking of birds in all directions and the swish of fresh flights as the ducks came in to feed. It was an experience I shall never forget and I was very grateful to the Wali for having given me the chance.

The guns had to wait for the Wali to open the firing. This is an unwritten law and appreciated by all shikari guests. After waiting for the light to improve the first bang went off and in a moment duck of different kinds were swooping about, disturbed and not quite knowing from which direction. At all heights and from all angles those duck passed by and I banged away at them to my heart's content. I only had one gun (which I had bought on my first home leave), a Westley Richards, that soon began to get warm and I had to allow some birds to pass by peacefully. The birds kept going and coming. Perhaps it was only the fresh flights that came once the firing had started, I can't say. I must have fired off a hundred cartridges by the time a halt was called by our host. By this time I was beginning to get a thick head so I was quite ready to cease fire and wait for the men to bring in the last of the shot birds. Our four guns had bagged nearly 200 duck, with the Wali getting the highest number of birds. I had watched him pick out some of the birds. He seldom missed a shot. A most charming host, he had not spared himself in giving the best that his small domain of Swat could offer and before we departed for home he presented each of us with a lovely warm Swattie *choga*,[4] ideal as a dressing gown. On a retiring commandant's last night in the Guides, he was the guest of honour in the Mess for dinner. The beautifully polished dining table, extended to full length for this special occasion, reflected the wonderful silver trophies and silver cutlery of which the Guides were so very proud. In no other Mess in India have I ever seen such a magnificent collection.

Every officer of the Corps, cavalry and infantry, was present to bid farewell to the Commanding Officer who had probably served thirty years in the Guides. What a dinner it was: hors d'oeuvres, soup, fish, roast, sweet and a savoury. Then the table was cleared and the wine was brought in by the mess havildar, and placed before the President at the head of the table: two decanters, one of port and the other of Madeira, also two large cut-glass jugs, one with whisky and the other with water for teetotallers. The same kind of set was placed before the Vice-President at the foot of the long table. The wine was then passed round from both ends and when every officer's glass was filled the President rose to his feet, tapped the table for silence and called out, 'Mister Vice-President, the King!' The Vice-President rose to his feet and replied, 'Gentlemen, the King Emperor!' Everyone then drank to the health of His Majesty. The wine was passed round a second time for glasses to be filled to drink the health of our chief guest. The next senior officer made a short speech and everyone drank to the health of the departing guest. Someone then broke into 'Auld Lang Syne' with all joining in and finishing up with 'For He's a Jolly Good Fellow'. The old band havildar was now invited to come in and sit by the President and was given a drink, while the Pipe Major and his next best exponent on the bagpipes took up their stand behind the guest's chair and played his favourite Scottish melodies. Everyone was in the best of spirits as the wine was kept circulating and after a spell they shouted 'Speech, speech!' until the guest was forced to his feet and made to say a few words, not a very easy thing to do for someone who is leaving his beloved regiment. After dinner the senior officers cut out for bridge while the rest of us went into the billiard room to play slosh, a kind of billiards, and afterwards dumb charades.

At twelve the party was still in progress when half a dozen subalterns went along to the infantry lines and trundled back an empty mule cart, of which every unit had ten for station duties. In front of the Mess verandah the cart was parked and a padded chair deposited amidships. A little later, when the guest rose to take his leave of the party, he was lifted up shoulder high, carried outside and deposited on the chair in the cart. Then amidst shouts and cheering the chariot was propelled along at breakneck speed until we arrived at his house, where he was carried to his front door and allowed to enter. All shouted farewell, and so ended a great party.

Our next move was to Razmak, Waziristan, where about ten years previously a very large standing camp for six battalions had been built. Razmak, with its shops, club, nice roads, gardens and many amenities was indeed more a cantonment than a camp. We moved there under the command of Pat Grant, our new Commandant. He was the last of our pre-First World War officers and with his quiet and efficient ways a most popular commanding officer with all ranks.

We moved by rail to Bannu after crossing the Indus at my old friend Kalabagh, then went by motorized transport along the new

148

Razmak road. We stopped halfway for the night at a battalion camp situated along the ridge of a rocky hill. Leaving most of our kit in the 3-ton lorries parked in the camp, we built ourselves sangars for safety and then spent the night in comfort. Early the next morning we were on our way again and after a few hours our convoy arrived at the head of the Razmak pass guarded by a strong permanent picquet of a company supplied by the Razmak garrison. Picqueting troops from Razmak always opened the road from the cantonment to the pass for weekly convoys bringing up supplies of fresh troops, for all units of the garrison were changed every two years.

It was in 1920 that I had last viewed the Razmak *raghza* from a mile or two towards Makin from Kaniguram. Now I looked down the valley, broad and inviting past Razmak and about 8 miles away lower down where Kaniguram reposed on her long ridge. Soon our motor convoy entered the guarded gate of Razmak and, passing through the cantonment, we came to a halt about 300 yards away at the southern end of the road. Our men soon unloaded the lorries and took the kit and stores into the different barracks, houses and store rooms. We found that all the buildings were first class, with water and electricity laid on. The solid structure of the whole camp must have awed the Mahsuds. They now knew for certain that the Army was there for keeps. How they must have regretted that they had not kept their part of the pact agreed upon in Kaniguram in 1920.

The Officers' Mess and quarters were most comfortable, the latter fully furnished. We had brought our own furniture and a new radiogram for the Mess, our share of the Corps' silver and trophies, carpets, curtains and so on, so that once we were settled in Razmak, our Mess was quite the most comfortable in the cantonment. Stuck away in Mahsud country for two long years we had made up our minds to make the stay as happy as possible.

Few picquets were required for the protection of Razmak because of its situation on the plain, and this meant that battalions were able to move out in good strength, leaving behind only a few men for guards and perimeter groups. Even so, sniping often took place at night and even once or twice during daylight. Hockey and football grounds were outside the perimeter and on one occasion, while I was having a practice game with our team, we were fired at from about 800 yards from low hills lying to the north-west. Judging from the number of bullets that went ricochetting into the air after striking the pitch, I should think that the Mahsud party responsible for spoiling our game consisted of probably twenty or more rifles. No one was hit, indeed it would have been very bad luck had anyone stopped a bullet. But we halted the game and ran back into the cover of our perimeter.

Hardly ever were our troops out on the *raghza* without the Mahsuds interfering, usually during the withdrawals, and generally then contenting themselves with long-range sniping, annoying but not very dangerous, although occasionally a man was hit. As the low hills from which these enemy fired were broken and had many bushes, it was most difficult to spot the snipers. All six battalions in the Brigade were well trained, good on the hills and gave the enemy few opportunities for their tactics. On one occasion, when our battalion was withdrawing after opening the road as far as the pass for the convoy, the Mahsuds followed up at long range and continued to worry us for a mile or two of our retirement. For transporting the Battalion's reserve ammunition mules were always allotted from the brigade transport corps, and with each mule an unarmed *drabi* (leader) came along.

In addition to the enemy who followed up along the plain, some commenced to bring harassing fire to bear on our men from the hills to the east of the route, which were not picqueted because of their distance from the motor road. Some of these distant riflemen made a dead set at our battalion's transport, frightening one of the *drabis* to such an extent that he dived into a convenient pit, probably an old shell hole, after he had let go of his animal's reins. One of our men collected the animal before it could run off home with its load of two boxes of SAA. All the transport was moved a couple of hundred yards to the west on the broad *raghza* where they were safer, but the frightened little mule-leader refused to emerge from his funk hole and our withdrawal was held up. The snipers, who were firing from the eastern hills, surely had a sense of humour. Every time that unfortunate young lad, not more than eighteen, popped his head up before making up his mind to run for it, bullets would throw up nasty spurts of dust a yard or two from him and he would go to earth again. I had arrived at the pit to try to encourage this Jack-in-the-box to make

150

a dash for home and safety but the Mahsud, who I feel sure were enjoying this tragic-humorous little drama, fired not a shot at me or my orderly who was with me. They concentrated their attention on the scared *drabi*, until eventually my orderly went down, yanked him out and ran with him to give him moral support.

On that day our battalion had the only casualty it suffered in the twenty or so times we were on a road-opening operation towards the Ramak Narai. He was the commander of my Sikh machine-gun section; he was badly disabled and never returned to serve after hospital.

In 1937, the Razmak Brigade Commander took out a column south towards Sarwekai, along a broad track that had been made by Mahsuds working under the guidance of our engineers. This road led past Kaniguram over the next ridge (which my Scouts in 1920 had held during the evacuation of our Waziristan Frontier Force from the Kaniguram plain), then on west and south through a heavily wooded area of valleys and high hills.

Right from the start the Guides got into trouble from a high rocky hill on our left, on which my B Company's Sikh platoon had established the first picquet. Enemy were on the hill but the Platoon had taken it without a casualty. However, a short while after a message came in that in an attack, one of the picquet had been killed and another wounded. It took six men to bring the casualties down from that steep and high peak and the reduction of eight rifles in one platoon left it rather thin, but the enemy had most probably also suffered for they did not attack again, and later in the withdrawal they did not attempt to follow up.

The Force moved on another three miles over the ridge and along the valley I have mentioned above. For some unaccountable reason, the commander decided to camp in the close valley for the night. Of all the many campsites in which I have been an occupant in trans-border operations, I would say without any reservation that this was the most dangerous and ill-selected. With the hillsides covered in stunted oak bushes and sweeping down to within a hundred or two hundred yards of where we bivvied that night, we could have been unmercifully sniped or even attacked had the Mahsuds so wished. Thank God, they did nothing and the next day a portion of the small force moved on. That was to be a day of tragedy for the Guides. With one battalion staying behind in that deplorable camp in the wooded valley, two battalions, a battalion of the famous Sikh regiment and one of the Guides, moved out and on towards our next and final camping ground.

The Sikh Battalion put up strong picquets on two or three hills and our turn came next to picquet a very thickly wooded hill that came down to the road from a great height on our left flank. This long ridge was about 300 yards beyond the last Sikh Battalion's company picquet but it was so long and high that it was impossible, and also unnecessary, to occupy the summit, which would have necessitated a battalion operation. The last Sikh picquet was only halfway up the long high ridge it occupied.

Pat Grant, our Commanding Officer, was with the General on a flat-topped hill, or rather a ridge to the right of the road watching our next company moving on. I happened to be nearby as my B Company was next for picqueting and I was also expecting orders from the Machine-Gun Company to go into action. A company under Campbell doubled forward in section groups towards the foot of the hill they were to occupy and, as I watched their progress through my binoculars, I saw, by chance, a strong party of tribesmen moving high up towards the summit of that same hill. Running up to the Commanding Officer I told him and asked for permission to take the Machine-Gun Company forward to cover A Company's advance. Leaving my B Company under command of my senior Indian officer, and taking our machine guns at the double, we moved up the long ridge occupied by the last picquet of the Sikhs and were soon in action protected by their men. I warned their Company Commander that enemy were about and, to prevent the tribesmen from interfering with A's advance, our eight guns began searching, with bursts of fire, the higher slopes of the hill so that they were able to get into their position without a casualty. The Sikh Company and our Machine-Gun Company men soon built themselves sangars in the thick bushes and I sent down all our mules as I was convinced that the enemy were still up on the hill, hiding amongst the trees. Our guns continued to fire bursts on the upper slopes of A's hill and this concentrated fire probably kept the enemy from attacking down towards them.

152

In the meantime, Pat Grant and John Redding, the Second in Command, had arrived and come up to our ridge to watch A Company's movements, but I was unaware that they were below me. Later John sent a runner up to tell me that the Commanding Officer had been badly wounded. I ran down at once to see him and find out what had happened. Apparently Pat Grant was standing on the ridge with three or four others, one of whom was my machine-gun subedar, a very tall Sikh, when the enemy opened fire suddenly on the group, felling three of them: Pat, my subedar and a third man. Before I arrived all three had been taken down the ridge for sending back to the Field Ambulance, but while John was telling me the details a runner came to inform us that Pat was dead. He had expired on the stretcher before getting to the ambulance. The others were not badly wounded but had to be evacuated. The sad point about it all was that Pat would not have been hit if he had heeded the warning I had given him and kept under cover. Why on earth stand in the open in a group when enemy are about? Nothing more happened and there was little firing. Perhaps the Mahsuds were satisfied with the toll they had extracted.

Campbell that day displayed considerable courage and initiative in his handling and leadership of his company, and once he had occupied the position with his usual thoroughness, he took out a strong patrol to search the jungle to the left and right of the road. I went along with his men and to our surprise we found an inhabited cave area situated in the midst of the forest on the right of the road and about a couple of hundred yards below. The women and children set up a howling, thinking that we would start slaughtering them. There were no men about and I imagine that the Mahsuds whom I had seen, and who had been responsible for our casualties, had come from this area. We left the village with the females and children still making a hullabaloo, rushing in and out of their caves in panic.

Only one or two more picquets were necessary to safeguard the route, so we settled down in our headquarters position and waited until the main body with the transport had passed through. We then moved down to a camping site only another mile or so further on, a sloping plain, and there we built our camp, safe from sniping for there was only one little hill overlooking our perimeter and on this knoll I commenced to build the camp picquet that we were to hold that night. John was not feeling well. I think the shock of losing dear old Pat had been too much for him and he had retired to his 40lb tent as soon as the pit had been dug for his bedding roll to be put in. That year, 1937, I was forty and John was quite ten years older. There was nothing much to do but supervise the building of the picquet and our own perimeter, and as the column had got in early we had lots of time before dark. After tea I was up on the knoll helping with the picquet and collecting rocks for the sangar when one of our men, swinging the end of a pick axe, loosened a huge round boulder that then started to roll down the gentle slope of the hill towards the camp, less than a hundred yards away.

The following incident, which may be hard for some readers to believe, is nevertheless Gospel truth: that large round rock, which must have weighed at least 600lb gathered speed and moved with unerring accuracy, as though guided by some unseen power, straight towards the 40lb tent where John slept. It broke through the unfinished perimeter wall which did not seem to break its velocity and went on to crash into the tent pole. The boulder disappeared and the near end of the tent collapsed. I was horrified and ran down after the rock, yelling to the men building the perimeter, 'Look out!' This they did, scattering in all directions. I was the first to arrive at the 40lb tent after racing along as fast as my legs could take me. One thought was repeating itself in my brain: 'Two commanding officers in one day, two COs in one day,' for I felt sure that John must be dead, squashed to pulp. Snatching aside the loose flap I gazed inside. 'Thank God!' I cried. John was safe. I found him sitting bolt upright at the far end of the pit with his legs tucked away under him. The near end of the pit was filled with the boulder. Blood was streaming down John's face from a deep cut on his forehead, made by the broken end of the tent pole striking him as it was thrown back by the impact of the stone. He could not say why, but some instinct had made him pull up his feet and body as the rock plunged into the pit where a fraction of a second before he had been stretched out.

John was not badly hurt and after an injection and the application of some plaster he was sent back to bed to sleep off the shock. What a day it had been and to crown it all that night a

154

violent rainstorm broke upon us, and flooded out our bivvies. It seemed as thought the heavens were sorrowing, mourning for our loss. However, the following morning the sun shone brightly and all kits were laid out to dry. Perhaps it was due to this terrific downpour that there was no enemy activity. The Mahsuds had vanished into their distant villages and caves. Not one was visible.

The object of the column's operation was now evident: another column from the recently built cantonment on the Wana plain had moved through Sarwekai and northwards to rendezvous with ours. Up to this time I had known nothing about this but the night before the storm I got a radio message from the Wana Colonel telling me that my brother was with it and would like to meet me the following day if the situation permitted. This was great news and I got permission to go across no man's land to try and get to his battalion headquarters, where we was temporarily in command of his battalion. And so two battalions of our 12th Frontier Force Regiment, the 3rd Sikhs and the Guides, met in the Waziristan hills after approaching from the north and south, many miles through hostile country.

Between our two columns there lay a Mahsud village and tower, the inhabitants of which had been involved in sundry attacks on our troops and the political people had decided that the village must be destroyed in reprisal. Our troops moved out to occupy the high ground from our side, while the Wana troops put up picquets from their end so that the village was surrounded completely.

Taking a section of my men I went across to meet my brother. This was one of the strangest meetings of two brothers, away in the heart of Mahsud land, possibly where no Britisher had been before. We shook hands, exchanged a few words for ten minutes, then parted as each of us had other work to do. We were indeed pleased to have been able to see each other, if only for a brief time. Surely God alone could have arranged that meeting.

The whole operation of surrounding the village and preparing it for demolition was faultlessly organized and accompanied in the minimum of time. After the demolitions the two columns separated and withdrew. This small and co-ordinated operation must have convinced those tribesmen amongst the Mahsuds who still held aggressive ideas that they could never count on remaining immune from retribution, however distant their village might be located.

But was it all worthwhile? In our battalion alone we had lost two killed (a lieutenant and a very junior sepoy) and three wounded (a very senior Indian officer, an NCO and a young sepoy). Of these five only the NCO would serve again. Other battalions possibly had like casualties, I don't know. On the enemy side I doubt whether they had more than one or two men hit. However, a tower and a few houses belonging to them had fallen in heaps and, having accomplished that big task, the following day we moved back towards Razmak.

Returning on the road we came by, with B Company plus the Machine-Gun Company and half a dozen signallers, I looked after the duties of rearguard for the column. Everything went along without a hitch until we got to the bend in the road where I had last spoken to Pat Grant the morning he was killed. The Sikh Battalion had a company picquet on this bend, that was located on a nasty densely wooded knoll. Because of the trouble the tribesmen had given us in this area during our advance, I was fully expecting some more during our withdrawal, especially as I knew the Mahsuds had that cave village within half a mile and, in addition, were probably determined to take revenge for the destruction of the village the day before. The rearguard troops and machine gunners were in a position to cover down the picquet that had been given the 'regiment to withdraw' order. They had acknowledged this and had come away fast, but had then disappeared amongst the lower bushes and I did not see them again. It was now the picquet commander's job to report in to the rearguard. Waiting for him to do this I was unable to withdraw my men as I was not sure that the picquet was safe. I became anxious as the delay to report in lengthened and delays in withdrawal in Frontier warfare are usually dangerous. Eventually the General himself came along and wanted to know why I was holding up the withdrawal. I replied that I was unable to retire further until I was convinced that the picquet had retired from the area safely. This I was trying to find out as it was my responsibility. He went off and in a short while I was sent a message to the effect that the picquet had reported in to the Adjutant of the Sikh Battalion lower down the road. Apparently it had dropped straight into the valley, moved along it for half a mile and then climbed up onto the road. On this occasion, because it happened that no enemy followed up the retirement, there were no serious consequences. But it might well have been otherwise. Also, it might have happened that I, as rearguard commander, would wish to keep back that company in my rearguard reserve. Every rearguard commander is fully entitled to do this, without referring to anyone else. This serious error on the part of the picquet commander left me with a ruffled temper, however, after that delay everything went along smoothly and we arrived back in the badly situated camp in the valley without further incident.

The next day we proceeded towards Razmak with the Guides acting as advance guard and putting up the route picquets. Nothing untoward occurred until the vanguard came to the area where five days before B Company's Sikh platoon had their casualties. The enemy were again on the same hill and peppered my vanguard pretty severely as we advanced up the Razmak *raghza*, but they did not wait to fight when an Orakzai platoon arrived near the hilltop. Those Pathans of B, led by an Orakzai platoon havildar, were a first-class fighting unit. Better I have never seen. The Razmak troops came out a little way to help us back and we entered our perimeter without experiencing any more trouble.

Back in Razmak we learnt that the body of our Commanding Officer had been flown back to be laid to rest in the Guides Chapel cemetery, by the side of his two young friends, Godfrey and Tony, who had died a few years previously in the Mohmand operations. Our next Commanding Officer, Towser Garret from the 1st Battalion of our group, had been detailed but was not to join us for a few weeks. In the interval John Redding was temporarily in command and I was temporary Second in Command.

The Mahsuds continued to trouble the Razmak garrison, generally on road opening days, and in one of these fights the 6th Battalion of the 59th Frontier Force Rifles had a running encounter from the Narai back to the cantonment, suffering half a dozen casualties. They then proceeded to interfere with the cantonment water supply from the west of the plain, where it was piped from a spring.

The Brigade Commander ordered out two battalions to attack two high features that overlooked the spring, where the enemy had taken up threatening positions. These two features were well within range of our howitzers and guns at Razmak itself, not more than a couple of miles distant. The Guides were to attack on the left and the other battalion on the right. The enemy must have had wind of our intention for they could be seen in force, their heads lining the crests of both the features and we knew that we were in for a good battle. Our objective was the summit of a 500-yard spur that ran down towards Razmak from the west, and the other objective was about 600 yards to the right. The eastern end of our preliminary objective ended in a very rocky knoll which we took with no opposition, and established ourselves firmly amongst the rocks that afforded good cover. Battalion Headquarters, with C Company in reserve and our Machine-Gun Company, remained here throughout the battle that followed.

The eight machine guns went into action behind strong sangars, ready to give intensive covering fire as soon as our A Company under young Campbell moved along the ridge to take up an inter-mediate supporting position, to be followed by my B Company (commanded that day by Ralph Griffiths, son of the Chief Commissioner of the North-West Frontier Province) which was to make the assault on the final crest. At zero hour the guns in Razmak opened fire on the two objectives for five minutes while our A Company rushed forward in extended platoon lines, under cover of our Machine-Gun Company which opened fire at the same time. So intensive was the fire that the enemy's heads disappeared from the crests of the objective, but they continued to fire on our position from a spur that branched off south from the final objective. In the meantime, the other battalion was making good headway towards their objective, under heavy fire. Within ten minutes A Company had taken their objective and began to establish themselves amongst the rocks. As soon as A Company were in position, B Company were to advance, supported by the covering fire of A Company and our machines guns. This was to continue until B Company made their final rush on to their positions, the crest of the hill.

While A Company were advancing, I had been directing the fire of the machine guns and it was then that I had one of the narrowest escapes of my life. I was sitting behind a large rock peering, luckily for me, through my binoculars, to see the strikes of the machine guns' traversing bursts when a sniper from the southern spur fired at me, but hit the end of the rock an inch or so under my chin. The blast, which was considerable, and the spattering pieces of rock and lead bowled me over onto my back, and for a second I thought I'd stopped a direct hit. However, I soon found that I was more shaken than injured and that there was not much blood on my face. My binoculars had saved my eyes. I ran to a safer sangar and removed my topee which I had foolishly been wearing, and put on the *safa*[5] my orderly carried for me. I hated wearing this *safa* on a hot day as it always left me with a headache.

Redding wanted me up front to ensure that the two forward companies were in strong and firmly established positions to repel any enemy counter-attack, and also to arrange the details of the withdrawal when the time came for the retirement. So I went behind B Company's rear platoon.

We passed to the right of A Company, keeping just below the edge of the long spur so as to be safe from enemy firing from their ridge. It was comforting to hear the staccato snap of our machine-gun covering fire as it passed a little above our heads, cracking the rocks all along the crest of our final objective. The big guns from camp had to stop their barrage for safety reasons when our leading platoon moved on past A Company, but the machine guns carried on. B Company took the crest in fine style and there the battle was hectic for some time. Enemy dead were lying about, most of them slain by the heavy fire of our howitzers. B Company soon had three casualties, only one of whom was seriously hurt. This unfortunate young NCO, a Sikh naik by the name of Munsha Singh, had been wounded only a few weeks before when on our last five-day expedition, and now he was back in hospital for several more weeks. However, I am glad to say that he recovered and rejoined to serve again. He was a grand lad and one of our battalion hockey players. Griffiths, who led the attack of B Company, was also hurt by a splintering bullet that left his face splattered with blood marks, but my young friend Ralph

Griffiths, a fine and courageous leader, carried on in front, setting a grand example to my B Company, which that day surpassed themselves in their dash and bravery. Dogras, Sikhs, Punjabi Militias and Pathans fought side by side, and the enemy were unable to shake them when they counter-attacked, having to withdraw and content themselves with long-range fire.

I imagine that the majority of the enemy in this fight were tribesmen from the Afghan side of the Durand Line, as they all appeared to be dressed alike in darkish clothing. But Afghans or Mahsuds, the tribesmen displayed courage and tenacity in the face of heavy and accurate fire from our side.

On our right the other battalion had moved along parallel to us and had had a hard fight. But they battled along firmly and achieved their objective just before we got to ours – there is no doubt that their presence on the hilltop, enabling them to fire onto the reverse slopes of our ridge, helped to keep the tribesmen from attacking us.

After a couple of hours the Force Commander ordered a withdrawal. The enemy obviously had had enough of the battle for they made no serious effort to follow up, as they usually did. I think the close, accurate covering fire deterred them. They were back on the crest a few minutes after B Company came away, but the guns and our machine guns kept them there and their heads down. B Company retired through A who, when B were safe behind Battalion Headquarters, then came in. There was no more firing from the enemy and from our side, just the occasional shell burst to warn the tribesmen against further action. After this short, sharp battle the Mahsuds quietened down and only once again, while we remained in Razmak, did our battalion have a skirmish with them.

A loop road, branching off from the main Bannu-Razmak metalled road about 10 miles back from Razmak and coming towards the *raghza* a little way south of the cantonment, was under construction and for many days our battalion moved out and was occupied in picqueting high hills protecting the work. Time and again B Company were sent up to occupy the same enormous feature and as I fully expected a battle one day, I varied my approach line and covering fire tactics as much as I could.

Strange to relate, the tribesmen never once interfered with these road-construction picqueting operations, although the hills were not far from the area where B Company had had their two small battles on the previous expedition on which our Commanding Officer was killed. I could only surmise that the political folk had either threatened with reprisals or heavily bribed the tribesmen of that area.

To cover the advance up the high features often necessitated our machine gunners deploying sections on other high ridges and crests, and on one of these operations a mule carrying ammunition boxes tripped, lost her footing and commenced to roll down the steep slope, not very fast, obviously out of self-control and with its legs held stiffly in the air when on her back on each roll. My men and I looked on aghast, unable to do anything. Crashing into a pine tree with a trunk about five or six inches in diameter, its frightening progress downwards was not lessened an iota. The tree merely snapped off about a couple of feet from the ground, and on and on she rolled until the bottom of the ridge was reached. Despatching an Indian officer and half a dozen men to retrieve the saddlery, boxes of small arms ammunition and crates, and with instructions to shoot the unfortunate animal if her back or a leg were broken, I went on with my work. Half an hour later my men were back with all the equipment after unsaddling the mule and, wonder of wonders, with the mule herself, walking placidly behind her leader. She was only scratched in one or two places and after a week's rest was back in harness. Her exploit spread abroad and she became the company mascot.

As the road neared completion, our battalion with another was sent out past the Razmak *marai*[6] and down the main road to the branching off spot to move along the new loop to a camping area about halfway along. With two companies of the Guides plus a section of guns of the British battery to form the rearguard of the small column, I had an interesting job that day. As far as the *marai* our protection was assured by other Razmak troops. The advance guard then put up picquets that were to be withdrawn by my rearguard.

About a mile down the road from the *marai* a few tribesmen commenced to worry the withdrawing picquets as well as the rearguard, and although this was more annoying than dangerous, for the enemy kept within four and six hundred yards from us, there was always the likelihood of a retiring picquet having a casualty that could easily lead to others. The gunner officer was with me and when I pointed out the hill from which some of the Mahsuds were firing, and when I asked him to clear them off, he wasted not a second. I could see all along that he and his lads were just longing to try out their beautiful new guns which I think were threes or 3.5s. He had a couple of signallers and as we walked along a telephone line was laid by his men from one of the two lorries ahead that transported the section of guns, the line being rolled in as we walked back down the pass. A few words down the phone and the guns came into action just off the road. Ramps in each lorry being let down from the rear enabled the guns to be manhandled in and out in a few seconds. Several rounds of shrapnel bursting accurately soon silenced the tribesmen.

The British lads were as excited as schoolboys and the efficiency with which they handled the guns was a delight to watch. They wanted other targets but I was anxious about my rearguard and getting in the picquets, so they had to rest content and come out of action. Within a few seconds the two trucks, which in the meantime had been hidden away, backed close to the guns that were then rolled along up and into the lorries. I withdrew to keep ahead of the rearguard.

The enemy kept quiet until the rearguard turned south along the new loop road when they, or another gang of tribesmen, commenced again to harass the withdrawal. This gave the section of guns another opportunity to have more live shell practice, which they were wanting and enjoyed to the full. The enemy ceased troubling us and the remainder of the withdrawal was uneventful. Our rearguard got into camp safely without having had a casualty, and the disturbances made by the enemy had been sufficient to keep our men on their toes.

The following day the Colonel returned by the same route. But this time a strong *gasht* of Tochi Militia *jawans* led by the re-doubtable Prendergast had moved out by night from Boya or Datta Khel towards us, waiting to catch those enemy in the rear if they tried any more tricks which, however, they didn't. They were clearly scared of being caught between two fires.

This was the last little operation the Guides were involved in while in Waziristan. A few days later Towser Garrett arrived to take over command from John Redding, who had carried out his command with great confidence and efficiency. But Towser, being the next senior officer in our 12th group after Pat Grant, had to get command. He was a fine soldier, we all took to him immediately and were very happy serving under him during the next two years.

While in the Training Battalion in Sialkot in 1932, I met an officer from our 14th Battalion who came to do the job of Adjutant. After he had completed his two years in the Training Battalion he had transferred to the South Waziristan Scouts, my old corps. One day Spider Keogh was motoring along the Sorarogha-Kaniguram new road when a Mahsud Khassadar, waiting round a bend, shot him dead at point-blank range – murder, for the sake of just murdering, and so another good friend of mine dead in Mahsud land. Shortly after, as our two-year tour was complete, another battalion was detailed to come and relieve us, so we packed up to vacate our lines, Mess and quarters for them, before returning to our home town of Mardan.

It was the custom in Razmak for the Officers' Club to throw a party for the officers of the outgoing battalion on their last night in Razmak. As I had run the hockey and football teams of the Battalion and had played in many friendly games against the different units' teams in Razmak, I had met most of the officers, with the result that they refused to accept a 'no' from me for this last-night spree. Ralph Griffiths, also a keen hockey player, and a couple of others came along with me to the Club. After an hour or two the atmosphere became hilarious and drink flowed freely. For those remaining in Razmak it did not matter much as the next day was a Sunday, but for us it was different for we would be loading into 3-ton lorries to be away by 7.00 a.m., and this meant getting up at 5.00.

The walls of the Club bar were hung with many polished shields, each about 14 inches by 12, for every major unit on leaving Razmak had its battalion or unit shield hung up according to the date of departure, and our shield was to take up its place that night.

Apparently our hosts had previously fixed on the time when the ceremony should take place, for with a shout of glee I was suddenly pounced upon and hoisted up onto the shoulders of a couple of stalwarts. The shield was thrust into my hands and amidst shouts of applause and the singing of 'Auld Lang Syne' I was carried round the room three or four times, then taken to the wall where in its appropriate place a hook had been placed on which our shield had to be hung. After several mishits, due I can assure you to the bucking antics of the two mounts and not to alcohol, I eventually was successful in completing the ceremony, after which I was unceremoniously deposited on the floor. We were at last able to take our leave of our guests who saw us out of the Club and called out their farewells as we made our way back to our rooms to get a few hours' sleep.

The next morning we departed from Razmak and its *raghza* and, after spending the night in the halfway camp we left Waziristan behind, for me forever. Altogether I had spent nearly ten years of my life in that dangerous and vile land, inhabited by a treacherous though brave people, possibly a record for a Britisher.

Back in Mardan under the leadership of Towser Garrett we were left in peace for many months. Clearly the powers in Simla realized that we had earned a long rest after our arduous two years of Razmak with the Mahsuds. Only the normal yearly round of company, battalion and brigade training took us out of our battalion centre. I was now acting Second in Command as all the officers senior to me had left, either on long leave or for attachment or secondment elsewhere. Staff work had no appeal for me and I was happy in the Regiment and with the men. On holidays I often took the battalion hockey or football team to Peshawar, Risalpur or Nowshera in our battalion bus to play friendly matches, or else invited other teams to Mardan. At weekends there would be polo to watch and there was always tennis available in the afternoon. We had four good grass courts and twice a year ran our own Mardan tennis tournament. Players were handicapped so as to encourage as many as possible to come over to enter.

In the winter there was shooting of a rough kind for anyone who was keen enough to look for it. Several small *jheels*[7] were to be found within five or six miles of the cantonment, and one could always reckon on bagging half a dozen snipe and a duck or two.

One of our pensioned Indian officers, the *malik* of his village, had much land, some of which included lowish hills. This area was not far from the village where Jack (the Assistant Superintendent of Police) and I, many years previously, had had our encounter with the Red Shirts. The Indian officer in question was a keen *shikari* and the portion of his estate that was cultivable was used by him as a private 'shoot'. He kept it well stocked with birds: chikoor, grey partridge and sisi. One fine day three of us were invited by him to enjoy *shikar*, shooting as well as hawking on his land. I was intrigued to see this hunting on the wing using trained hawks. Never before had this opportunity come my way, although, of course, in Baluchistan where I had spent my boyhood, I had many times seen wild hawks in action. The smaller ones, kestrels and sparrow hawks usually hunted the larks and field rats, while the larger and swifter falcons went for the blue rock pigeon. Our host had a small guesthouse that he kept spotless and where he entertained his friends. We spent the night there and enjoyed a wonderful feast of delicious lamb pilao, ending up with nuts and then lovely apples and oranges. Pathans are great ones for eating different kinds of nuts, most of which come down the Khyber Pass from Afghanistan, the favourite being *chilgozers*, walnuts, almonds and pistachio nuts.

The following morning the *shirkar* started off with falconry and we made a line with beaters and guns, although the host asked us not to shoot until the hawks had finished their demonstration. I felt that he was nervous of one of the guns mistaking his pet hawk for a grey. We walked up a level bit of ground between two ridges. The whole area was fairly well covered in thick thorn bushes, the average height of which was about five feet. Two hawks were out, one a beautiful, fierce-looking falcon and the other a small bird that was brought along for an outing as it was yet not fully trained. The big bird was unhooded as we went along slowly, with the beaters throwing stones into the bushes to flush the partridge, and it was not long before a covey broke out and scattered in all directions. The falcon selected his bird and was off like a streak of lightning. I don't think that victim ever knew what had struck it like a thunderbolt, and it was probably dead by the time the hawk brought it to the ground and sat with it in its needle-sharp talons. He permitted his trainer to remove his kill and was immediately rewarded with a titbit of some sort. After three or four kills the grey, petrified, refused to be flushed and a frightened bird preferred to have a beater pull it out of a bush than risk being struck down within 20 yards by its terrifying predator. Only one bird that the falcon pursued escaped sudden death. It got up about 30 yards ahead when our party had arrived at the top of one of the ridges. It was a large chikoor and made off at terrific speed down towards the valley with the hawk in hot pursuit and gaining rapidly. But when the hawk was within 10 or 15 yards of him he dropped like a stone into one of the very thick thorn bushes and hid. The falcon, braking suddenly, took a perch on a branch of the bush and waited for his trainer to come and either haul out the chikoor or flush it again. But that chikoor got away. Clearly he had sneaked off through the thick undergrowth and then made off as fast as his legs could carry him, and a chikoor can run very fast. There was no bird to be found in that bush when we arrived down and I was glad Mr Chikoor had got away.

With the hawks still out, although hooded and therefore not working, it was hopeless trying to shoot, for the birds refused to rise when they knew a hawk was in the offing, or else they got up reluctantly when the bushes they were hiding in were beaten with long sticks. They were then so close that shooting was not fun. Having watched this kind of *shikar* once left me with no desire to repeat the experience.

Once the hawks had been sent home and we arrived at a fresh bit of ground the shooting was first class, but battling one's way through the thorn bushes was a most painful undertaking and it wasn't until I got into a hot bath that night that I realized how many nasty scratches I'd collected in the excitement of the chase.

It was about this time that things began to hot up in Europe and the Second World War began. All British officers had to be medically checked for service overseas. About eight or nine of us were present with the Battalion at that time and our medical officer, Doherty, who had been awarded a DSO on the day of our action against the Mohmands for conspicuous gallantry in attending to our wounded when under heavy fire, examined each of us in turn. With the exception of one officer, we all passed his scrutiny. The officer who failed was Duncan, 'Duncy' to all of us, an Australian. He was one of the most popular officers in the Indian Army. Doherty was aghast when he examined Duncy's throat and ordered him off to the British military hospital, Peshawar. He then broke to us the dreadful news that our brother officer would be dead within a month and that nothing could save him. The medical officer's prognosis proved accurate and a few days later news came from Peshawar that Duncy was dead. A blood vessel in his throat had burst and he had passed away in a few seconds. His body was brought back for burial in our Guides cemetery. It will be impossible for anyone who attended that funeral to forget the sad event. Hundreds of friends came from Peshawar, Nowshera and Risalpur to pay their last respects to a very gallant officer. When a subaltern serving with the Australian forces in Gallipoli in the First World War, he had been decorated with the DSO and two bars, and also the Military Cross. Eight of us young majors of the Corps of Guides bore the coffin from the chapel to the grave, not very far away, for the cemetery surrounded the church. There wasn't a dry eye amongst us while the service was being conducted and as we carried him to the side of the grave. Our dear friend's body was laid alongside that of Pat. Dear old Duncy, he was first and foremost an Australian, after that a member of our armed forces. At no time was this more evident than when, with his attention glued to the mess radio, he listened to the details of a match between the MCC and the Australians taking place in Sydney. As his idol, Donald Bradman, scored four after four and looked like staying in until doomsday, Duncy's face would gleam with pride. And as the foregone conclusion of the match came over the air, he would gloat over us. It was his victory. How we missed him – he left a gap in our battalion that no one else could fill.

Beyond this sad episode, at that time life in Mardan continued to be peaceful for the Guides and it wasn't until the war had been on for a few weeks that we were moved again. This time we marched to relieve a battalion in Fort Bara on the Khajuri plain. The Commanding Officer was unwell and it fell to my lot to command the Guides, the last time I marched with them out of my home town of Mardan. We did the move in three easy stages: the first day to Nowshera, the second to Peshawar and the third to our new fort, Bara, which gets its name from the river that flows through the Khajuri plain after coming out of the Afridi hills some miles west. This fort, rather like Jamrud, was huge and had ample accommodation for a battalion. The officers had comfortable rooms and Mess, and the men's lines were not too cramped. Here we stayed for some dreary weeks with little to occupy our time but parades. Peshawar was within easy reach and so long as a minimum of five officers remained in the fort at weekends, the rest of us were able to go and enjoy the many amenities available there.

After a couple of months orders came from Division for me to proceed to Landi Kotal and conduct a mountain warfare course for thirty officers of the Brigade. I asked for a fortnight in which to prepare my lectures and exercises, and this was allowed me. It was barely enough and I had to work hard to get ready in time.

Previous to this I had never been called upon to give lectures to other officers and, although I understood my subject, considering all the experience I'd had in Waziristan, I started off rather nervously. However, a couple of days helped to banish my shyness and with the brigade officer helping me with the issuing of notices, the cyclo-styling of my lectures and arranging transport for my class when exercises took us far afield, I managed to get through the course without boobing too much. I must say I enjoyed my three weeks in Landi Kotal after the boredom of Bara, for I had been given nice quarters and fed in the very comfortable Brigade Mess.

On my return to Bara I found that many changes had taken place in the Indian Army. As a result of the war, new units and formations were in the building and to our distress (but most probably to his joy) Towser, our Commanding Officer, was ordered off to command a brigade somewhere east of India. By this time I had served on the books of the Guides longer than any other officer, but four of them were senior to me in service. However, three of these had recently left for good on transfer to other jobs and this left Richardson, six months senior to me as next for commanding officer after Towser. I had hardly met him for in the past ten or fifteen years he had been most of the time away on seconded jobs. He hastened back to take command and within a month of his return I was detailed to raise and command a new Frontier Force Battalion assembling in Assam.

To form this new unit, drafts of about a hundred men were sent along from each of our regular battalions, and to bring us up to authorized strength a large party of newly trained recruits arrived from the Training Regiment, Sialkot. Officers detailed from the Assam battalions also reported for duty and in a fortnight we were hard at work organizing our new Frontier Force Battalion. I was very lucky in that I was given as Second in Command a great friend and most efficient officer, who took half the heavy burden off my shoulders. My Adjutant also was most efficient and I was fortunate in being able to keep him in the Battalion for more than a year, by which time we were fully trained and in perfect trim to take our place in any Frontier Brigade. I of course knew that my Second in Command would not be left with me for long. He was too good to be spared and after six months, during which time he had organised our office, promotion lists, accounts section and many other important details, he left to take command of his own battalion. My thanks and gratitude towards him will never be sufficient for all the hard work, energy and above all unstinting loyalty he gave me in my uphill job. The raising of a new battalion is anything but easy. The taking over command of a regular battalion of the same group is easy in comparison.

After six months we were railed back to the North-West Frontier, from where we had all come, and I often wonder why we had not been allowed to form in the Frontier Province. Surely that would have saved the Government thousands of rupees. To rejoin my battalion I had left the Khajuri plain and it was here that I returned, for our first Frontier assignment was the guarding of

Fort Sallop and Jhansi post on the Afridi tribe border. We were able to get on with our training, being left in peace with never even a single brigade inspection to disturb us. After six months on the plain we marched up to Landi Kotal to be included in the Brigade. By this time we were a smart and efficient unit and to help me I had a fine lot of officers, half of them Indians, a most happy crowd on the whole. I was indeed lucky in having such a fine battalion.

About a year previously my brother had been transferred from his unit to command our 2nd Battalion serving in Malaya, and one day I received the frightening news that he was missing and believed killed. My little old mother wrote to me in agony of spirit and I sent back the only reply I could think of: 'Pray, pray to our Heavenly Father that all will be well.' God, in His mercy, answered our request in a miraculous way, for my brother escaped the clutches of the Japs and, with all of his officers, got away in a boat. They landed on a friendly island and eventually got back to India to be able to serve again. Shortly afterwards I got another message from Simla to the effect that our King had been pleased to award him the Victoria Cross. I was thrilled at the news, probably more than he was.

A few months later an order arrived for me to proceed overseas immediately to join a battalion serving in Egypt, in the Western Desert at El Alamein. This was indeed a nasty shock for me. With a dash of a pen, I was made to leave the battalion I had raised and trained with such care for Frontier warfare, to join a completely strange unit in quite another group and involved in desert fighting. Within two days I packed, handed over and was ready to leave for Karachi. What a wonderful farewell my officers and men gave me and it cheered me to know that they had been happy under me. I had my car, intending to drive down to the railway station where I was to catch my train in the afternoon to Peshawar. But I was not permitted to drive. On emerging from my room I found that ropes had been tied to the front buffer. All my officers dragged my little Austin, with me in it, all the way down that long road that was lined by my men who shouted their farewells as I was taken past. I was indeed sad to leave – life in the Army can be difficult at times.

At Peshawar I was taken to a creek, on the waters of which floated a spick and span-looking flying boat. My companion for the voyage was already sitting in a small rowing boat waiting for me and in a minute we were being taken along to climb into the Catalina. The engines roared for some time before we raced down the creek, then skimmed the water to become airborne, gain height and make our way over the Arabian Sea for a few hours to touch down at a small island on the north-east coast of Arabia. After refuelling we went on our way to fly over Mesopotamia and later to come down on to the Dead Sea's placid waters. I had often wished to see Palestine and this floating visit (for after a night in a hotel we flew on to Egypt) merely whetted my desire. The following day we alighted on the Nile at Cairo and were taken along to a posh hotel where we parked ourselves for a few days until the Army was ready to send us along into the Western Desert to join our respective units.

My station wagon came from the Battalion to fetch me and for several hours we ploughed along slowly through the sand, passing on the way many units belonging to our Desert Army. Eventually we arrived at El Alamein where I was directed to the battalion I was to command. In the Mess, dug deep into the sand, I met my officers, all Britishers, all tough-looking lads. After a meal and half an hour's rest I got my Second in Command to pile into my armoured carrier and show me round the companies, all dug in to very deep trenches for protection against heavy gunfire. The area the Battalion was responsible for defending was considerable, so much so that one company was out of touch with the next. But in a desert where everything is extensive I suppose that couldn't be helped. However, I did not like it. I had been taught differently. Some of our trenches had been dug into solid rock; to move would have meant a colossal amount of work and would have taken a long time.

Our battalion was at the south end of the front line, which extended from the Mediterranean Sea southwards into the desert. Only one other battalion, a British one, was south of us and beyond that was the empty expanse and then the Kalai Depression, a few rock outcrops but mostly sand, sand, sand. I asked Hugh, my Second in Command, why it had been necessary for an officer from a formation other than their own to have been brought in to command, and he explained that they had run short of senior officers. They had suffered many officer casualties, including two commanding officers killed. Actually I could not understand why he should not have been given command for he was fairly senior with fourteen years' service, knowledgeable and, which was more to the point, he really understood this type of warfare.

The men were first-class and their Pathan Company[8] were specially glad to see me. But I soon came to know that all was not as it should have been with the Punjabi Militias. There had been some mix-up with promotions and a certain element amongst them was disgruntled. I put a committee of Indian officers on to sorting out the difficulties, but they were not very successful. Apparently promotions in the depot in India had been made without taking into consideration our men facing the dangers in the front line. This was a legitimate moan but difficult to solve where thousands of miles separated the Battalion from the Depot.

Besides occasional shelling there seemed to be little enemy activity. Only once did bullets fall where I happened to be standing, and that was when I watched a dogfight between a German plane and one of ours above our lines. I could hear the rattle of the machine guns firing at each other and it was some of these bullets that happened to fall close by. Once or twice I went forward into no man's land for a recce in my carrier but was not fired at, although the enemy there could not have been more than 800 yards away. Perhaps they were trying to bluff us into thinking that they weren't there, for not long afterwards it was on this flank that Rommel made his thrust.

However, they bluffed no one and when they came in their tanks to sweep round our left they found our armour waiting for them, and not many of theirs returned to tell the tale. We knew well enough that something was coming, for that night was turned into day by thousands of flares that kept floating down from the dark sky. Their artillery barrage was severe but as our troops were well dug in we escaped lightly. I got a message from my Intelligence Section forward that one of the companies of the battalion on our left had fallen back and this, I feared, would leave our Pathan Company rather dangerously open on their left front. I went along in my carrier with the Sergeant Major to check up, but I was glad to find that they were in good heart. They assured me that nothing would shift them. I moved off to return to my headquarters and was nearly blown up on the way. When several heavy shells commenced to come over we stopped and, after jumping out of the vehicle, flung ourselves flat on the sand. However, no one was hit, not even my carrier, but we waited until that heavy barrage lifted to pound the sand dunes further back.

The Italians and Germans lost that battle and the next stage of the war was dictated by Monty. Nothing stopped his fine army as they pushed on and on to victory. Our line was left behind and as the war went further and further to the west, the danger to Alexandria and Cairo diminished. After a few weeks our brigade was moved across the Suez Canal through Palestine and the desert of North Arabia to finish up in a huge camp outside Baghdad. Here we were stuck with nothing to do but twiddle our thumbs.

As there was no real need for me to be with the Battalion during the move to Baghdad, I had asked permission and obtained it to go ahead. I was very keen to see some of the Holy Land and this seemed to me to be a heaven-sent opportunity. Crossing the bridge at Ismalia I motored in my station wagon along to Jerusalem, visited Bethlehem, the Mount of Olives and many of the churches dotted about. Then I went on to Samaria and further north to Nazareth, and from the high ground above the lake of Gennessaret I had a wonderful view of the country. Nearly 2,000 years previously, Christ must have looked down several times on the same picture. Traversing Arabia to the east I came to Baghdad, having been on a wonderful trip, which I shall never forget.

Those many days I had spent in the Western Desert, combating the myriad of flies (surely a plague that Moses had called down on Pharaoh and that he had subsequently forgotten to lift) had, I feel sure, resulted in my contracting some nasty malady and during the months that followed I lost weight rapidly, until eventually the medical people decided to return me to India. With hundreds of others I boarded a troopship at Basra and we steamed down the Persian Gulf, eventually calling at a small desert port on the eastern coast of Arabia. My cabin companion happened to go ashore and, after meeting some Air Force officers, returned to the ship with the astonishing news that a Catalina would be flying that day to Karachi and that they would be pleased to take along two officers and a little kit. I was all for accepting this heaven-sent opportunity. We got permission from the Commanding Officer of the ship, packed our few belongings and hurried ashore in time to get to the jetty where the Catalina was ready to start. We had just managed to catch her.

These aircraft flew daily over the Arabian Sea to keep a watch out for Jap submarines that were beginning to be active in the Indian Ocean, but the sea on that day was completely empty of shipping of any sort. After a few hours we approached the Makran coast and continuing along, soon caught sight of Kiamari, which we passed over, coming down in the same little creek from which I had left a few months earlier. This time the water was turbulent and, believe it or not, I was seasick in the horrible little rowing boat that took us ashore. But I expect this was due to my ill health. After reporting our arrival at Headquarters Karachi we awaited further orders.

The following day I went along to the British military hospital as I felt unwell, and the medical officer, after giving me a thorough examination, informed me that my trouble was most probably due to my teeth, which were in a bad state. He advised me to have them out, so they were all removed. Whether it was the type of injection that had been given me or the loss of blood in my already weak condition, I am unable to say, but when I awoke the following morning I was paralysed below the waist. To move my body was agonizing, to sit up was impossible. I was really frightened and phoned, or rather asked someone to phone, the British military hospital and ask for a doctor to come over. After fifteen days' treatment I was able to walk and was put on different kinds of treatments at the hospital until my general condition gradually improved. When I was considered fit enough, and at fortnightly intervals, I was brought before three medical boards, each consisting of three doctors. The first two boards were not able to come to any decision, but at the third board I was declared to be unfit for further active service. My treatment continued for several more weeks and, although I never fully recovered, I was put into a soft job for the remainder of the war.

And so I ended my service sad because I was unfit, yet most of my memories are glorious and happy, for it has been my very great privilege to serve for many years in peacetime, and in several wars, alongside the truly magnificent soldiers of Frontier militias and the Indian Army, surely a fighting force second to none in the world.

Notes

Chapter 1

1. Quetta was ceded to the British by the Khan of Khelat in 1875. The city derives its name from the Pashto word *Kawkot*, or fort. Lying outside the North-West Frontier Province but still dominated by a Pathan majority, Quetta is the capital of Pakistan's Baluchistan province. Quetta lies on the road to the Afghan city of Kandahar via the Bolan Pass, second only in strategic importance to the Khyber Pass. The British Army twice used Quetta as an invasion route to Afghanistan, during the First and Second Afghan wars of 1839 and 1878, respectively. The city later gained prominence as the seat of the British Staff College, founded in 1907. Much of Quetta was destroyed by an earthquake in 1935. As a result of its proximity to Afghanistan, thousands of Mujahedin fighters poured into Quetta during the Soviet invasion of 1979, turning the city into a centre for arms and drugs smuggling.
2. Havildar: the equivalent of a British Army sergeant major.
3. [Lieutenant Colonel Arthur Cumming VC.]
4. Baluchistan: one of Pakistan's four provinces, lying alongside the Afghan border south of the North-West Frontier Province. The inhabitants of this arid, mountainous region are mostly members of the Baluch and Pathan tribes. Baluchistan, whose capital city is Quetta, came into existence with the arrival from Iran of the Baluch tribes, probably around AD 1000.

5. Cantonment: a military station in India at the time of the Raj. The cantonments were usually built on a plan that is originally that of a standing camp, or 'cantonment'. The most notorious was the compound of bungalows and barracks erected by the British in Kabul following the 1839 invasion of Afghanistan and occupation of that city. The complex where the British had foolishly chosen to hold up, instead of behind the secure hilltop walls of the Bala Hissar citadel, was to prove almost indefensible against attacks once the insurrection began that eventually drove the army out of the city to its doom on the march back to India.

6. *Poshtin*: sheepskin coat.

7. *Kiloor*: small mammal inhabiting the desert regions along the Afghan border.

8. Shikari: sportsman, usually applied to a hunter.

9. *Garry*, also *gharry*: a cart or carriage.

10. Frontier Force: a special force called the Guides was raised in 1846 by Lieutenant (later Sir) Harry Lumsden to combat the problem of tribal incursions into the so-called settled districts of the North-West Frontier. The Corps originally consisted of one troop of cavalry and two companies of infantry. The Guides did not wear the traditional army red jackets but a new colour called khaki, a Hindi word meaning 'dusty' or 'dust-coloured', which was to become the symbol of armed forces throughout the world. The Guides were later expanded to become the Frontier Force Regiments, known to this day as the Piffers.

11. Administrative Border: the land from the Indus to the line of the North-West Frontier Province that was under direct British rule and which runs along a north-south axis adjoining the tribal territory known as the Federally Administered Tribal Areas (FATA). This area is governed by tribal law although it was nominally a part of British colonial (and now Pakistani) territory.

12. Mahsud: the Mahsud of Waziristan are generally acknowledged to be the most warlike and recalcitrant of the Pathan tribes. The tribesmen's obsession with revenge and terrifying predilection for cruelty were the two traits that stood out in the minds of British veterans of the Frontier.

13. Nullah: a dry river bed or ravine, often quite deep and wide, that was routinely used by the tribesmen as an escape route after a raid on a police post or Frontier town.
14. *Jawan*: a private solider or in some cases a constable.
15. *Dushman*: in Urdu, 'enemy'.
16. Sir George R.K.: Sir John Donald was a comparatively minor figure in the pantheon of Frontier administrators, but Major General Sir George Roos-Keppel, of British-Dutch descent, was one of the greats who answered to the role model of the soldier-scholar, in the tradition of Alexander. The Khyber Rifles Commandant had written a grammar of the Pushtu language, and was a prolific academic who translated arcane Pushtu works, such as the *History of Sultan Mahmud of Ghazni*. Roos-Keppel served as President of the Government's Committee of Examinations in the Pathan Language. Such was his passion for Pathan culture that he co-founded Islamia College, a sumptuous grouping of red sandstone colonial buildings in a setting of palm groves, that is now the undergraduate school of Peshawar University.
17. The Pathans' three most coveted possessions are usually referred to as *zar, zan, zamin* – wealth, women, land. The author substitutes 'water' for 'land' and this is quite plausible in Waziristan where he served, an arid region of the Frontier where water rights can often be the cause of blood feuds.
18. Baddi: this is more traditionally called *badal*. The Pathan lives according to a code of honour called *Pakhtunwali*. Life on the Frontier is governed by this tribal code, under which each man is bound to abide by three precepts. The first rule is that fugitives must without question be granted safety in one's home. Similarly, the Pathan is obliged to grant hospitality to all who seek it, friend or foe. However, the visitor should be forewarned that while he can rest easy while under a Pathan's roof, he is considered fair game as soon as he steps foot outside the door. Lastly, there is the law of revenge, or *badal*, the most sacred of the Pathans' three principal maxims. This normally takes the form of blood feuds, often inherited from past generations, arising from murders, violations of safe conduct or disputes about debts, inheritance or tribal quarrels over land or water.

178

19. Lance naik: equivalent to lance corporal in the British Army.
20. Piquet: a stone breastwork erected on a hilltop, along a ridge or other strategic spot to prevent sniping on a caravan or military convoy.
21. South Waziristan Militia: this later became the South Waziristan Scouts, a corps separate from the Tochi Scouts, which today retains its separate identity as one of the native levies raised by the British, and later expanded by Pakistan. The recruits are native Pathans from the Frontier whose role is to guard the tribal areas. The first of these corps was the Khyber Rifles, raised in 1878.
22. Wazir: the Wazirs, along with the Mahsuds, are the two dominant tribes of Waziristan. Their ferocity in battle is second only to the feared Mahsuds.
23. Malakand: the author served in this northern area of the Frontier less than twenty years after a famous field force was formed by the magnificently named General Sir Bindon Blood, to quell a revolt of the Pathan tribesmen. A young subaltern who covered this campaign as a war correspondent for the *Daily Telegraph* was Winston Churchill.
24. *Dak* bungalow, *khansama*: a *dak* bungalow is an Indian resthouse for the accommodation of travellers, and the *khansama* its caretaker.
25. Tonga: a light and small two-wheeled vehicle.
26. Chowkidar: watchman.
27. Suleman Khel Powindahs: the Powindahs are nomads of Afghan origin who each winter would drive their camels, mules and cattle down to the warm and fertile pastureland of the Indus valley. The Suleman Khel are a Powindah clan.
28. *Yakdan*: woven Afghan saddle-bag
29. *Mahseer*: a large river fish of the *Barbus* species, and highly prized by Indian anglers.

Chapter 2

1. *Gasht*: this was one of the native Scouts' favourite activities. The *gasht* is a routine patrol, carried out on foot or horseback as an exercise in 'showing the flag'.
2. *Chaplies*: lightweight boots of native manufacture.

3. Tiloor: various small birds, including local species of partridge and bustard.
4. Viper of Egyptian origin.
5. Syce: a groom, in common usage in Bengal.
6. *Gur*: a Bengali sweet.
7. *Gurguri*: thorn bushes.
8. *Mastare*, etc.: tribal greetings.
9. *Lashkar*: a tribal armed force.
10. *Pakhal*: water container, also cooked rice soaked in water.
11. Durbar: this can be used to mean a state occasion (such as the Edward VII's Coronation Durbar held in India in 1911), a court or a public hearing.
12. Civil and Military Gazette: the paper on which Rudyard Kipling worked as sub-editor in 1882
13. Chief Commissioner: Sir George Roos-Keppel.
14. Charpoy: a light bedstead.
15. Bunyah: in the Moslem provinces, a corn-dealer.
16. Ghee, atta, dhal: clarified butter, flour, split pulses, all Indian food staples.
17. *Narai*: plain.
18. *Rissala, Rissaldar*: a corps of native horse, a native cavalry commander.
19. Dera Ismael Khan: the main town of the southernmost tribal district, bearing the same name, of the North-West Frontier Province.
20. *Bahaduries*: plural of *bahadur*, military honours bestowed on native soldiers.
21. *Maidan*: an open space, in or near a town.
22. *Khattak*: Afghan folk dance.

Chapter 3

1. This is the *jezail*, a powerful, long-barrelled matchlock accurate to about 500 yards. It out-gunned anything the British or Indian armies put into the field until the advent of the Martini-Henry rifle in 1874. A Frontier officer once described the discharge of this elaborately ivory-inlaid musket as 'a rattling and banging, as of a minor train accident'.

180

2. Subedar: (also Subahdar), sepoy rank of company officer.
3. *Khajawa* stretcher: a pair of litters slung over the backs of camels, one hanging from either side.
4. Wallah: from the Hindi suffix *vala* (doer) and with reference to a person's role, as in box-wallah, an office worker. Roughly equivalent to English 'type'.
5. In this throwaway remark, Cumming unwittingly encapsulates the fatal flaw in Frontier policy. From the Raj's first contact with the Frontier tribes in 1839, until the Last Post was sounded in the Khyber Pass in 1947, the Government of India consistently treated the tribesmen of this remote corner of its Indian Empire as a military rather than an economic problem. Olaf Caroe, the last British Governor of the North-West Frontier Province, was once confronted by an Army officer serving in Peshawar, who expressed outrage at atrocities committed by the recalcitrant and warlike Pathans. Caroe replied that if in 1940 Hitler had been successful in his attempt to invade England, he hoped that every man in Britain would have fought the invaders with the same savagery as the Pathans against the British.
6. Tangi: gorge or ravine.
7. The other face of the Pathans was the extreme loyalty they could show to their British officers. Cumming more than once makes reference to incidents in which Pathan recruits risked their lives to save their commanding officers, including on one occasion Cumming himself. Firm and decisive leadership was the key to winning the minds and hearts of these ferocious tribesmen.
8. Pugaree: turban.
9. Tahsildar: officially, the chief native revenue officer of a sub-division of a district. In this case, the term refers to an agent attached to the military to reconnoitre the terrain.

Chapter 4

1. The standard British retaliation to outrages committed by the Pathan tribesmen was the 'butcher and bolt' policy. The Army never attempted to set up permanent garrisons in

tribal territory, but punitive expeditions were often sent in to inflict economic damage on the offenders, by torching and demolishing their villages and burning their crops. If this took place close to the onset on winter, before the villagers had time to rebuild their homes and resow the fields, the outcome was usually quite dire for the tribes.

2. Dogras: the Dogras of the hill regions of Himachal Pradesh, Punjab, Jammu and Kashmir have a long tradition of soldiering. They had been in the service of the British some years as part of the Frontier Force. The Dogras formed into a regiment in 1887 and three Dogra regiments were raised as part of the Bengal Infantry. During the World Wars, more Dogra battalions were added and after 1947 the Dogra Regiment formed part of the Army's post-1962 expansion.

3. Marwaties: Marwati Mountains in Katwaz, Afghanistan. It was historically the home of the Marwat tribe, whose name is derived from the Arabic *murrawat*, meaning compassion, generosity and manliness.

4. Kattaks, etc: Pathan tribes of the Frontier.

5. *Badraga*: the escort that accompanies a traveller through tribal territory.

6. *Sarai*: a resting place, more commonly *serai*, as in *caravanserai*, an inn with a central courtyard which served as an overnight stopover for camel caravans between Central Asia and India.

7. Palao: usually rendered as pilau, a rice of the Basmati variety grown in the Himalayan foothills and flavoured with sultanas, pine nuts, saffron and other spices.

8. SSO: senior staff officer.

9. 'Pindi: Rawalpindi, the twin city to Islamabad, although unlike the austere and antiseptic capital of Pakistan, from which it is separated by 15 miles of motorway, Rawalpindi is a bustling market city with miles of bazaars and shopping centres.

10. Black Mountain: between 1868 and 1891 the British fought three major campaigns against the tribes that inhabit the Black Mountain region in what is today the northern district of Pakistan's North-West Frontier Province.

Chapter 5

1. Khudai Khitmatgaran: the 'Red Shirt' movement was a Pathan nationalist organization of the North-West Frontier that closely followed Mahatma Gandhi's principles of non-violent resistance to British rule. In fact, the agitators frequently engaged in street clashes with the police. The Khudai Khitmatgaran flourished in the 1930s under the charismatic leadership of Abdul Ghaffar Khan, a giant of a tribesman who advocated a separate Pathan state known as Pakhtunistan. The movement died out following the creation of Pakistan in 1947.
2. Lathi: police baton.
3. Afghan war: the reference is to the Second Afghan War of 1878–1880.
4. *Choga*: a long-sleeved Afghan garment, like a dressing gown.
5. *Safa*: a tightly-wound cloth turban.
6. *Marai*: Cumming's use of the word appears to designate a district or perhaps a wooded area. The term *marai* is of Tamil origin and designates something hidden from sight, or preserved as a great treasure away from public gaze.
7. *Jheel*: a waterhole used by waterfowl.
8. Pathan Company: a Pathan unit called the Afridi Battalion was raised on the North-West Frontier when the Second World War broke out.

Bibliography

Primary Sources

British Library Oriental and India Office Collection (OIOC)

OIOC, *Report of the Indian Statutory Commission*, HMSO, London, 1930, vol. I, p. 102.

OIOC, *Report Showing the Relationship of the British Government with the Tribes Independent and Dependent on the North-West Frontier of the Punjab*, 1856, MF1/20 (microfiche), p. 55.

OIOC, Selections from the Records of the Government of the Punjab (New Series No. XIV), V/23/343, 1871–82, pp. 11–16.

OIOC, *North-West Frontier Policy*, L/MIL/17/13/11, 1920.

OIOC L/PS/18/A54/3 *Secret Correspondence between the Amir and the Viceroy*, 31 January 1885.

OIOC, *Parliamentary Papers, 1898* (C. 8714), Appendix G, p. 39.

OIOC, *Official History of Operations on the North-West Frontier*, 1882.

OIOC, *Supplementary Despatches of Duke of Wellington*, vol. IV, pp. 592–601.

OIOC, L/MIL/17/13/19, 1920, p. 388.

OIOC, *Debate in the House of Lords*, 7 March 1898.

OIOC, L/PS/10/45, Secret Papers, Letter from the Viceroy to the Amir Habibullah Khan, 10 May 1907, p. 86.

OIOC, Roos-Keppel, George, correspondence with the Viceroy in *North-West Frontier Policy*, 1920.

OIOC, Curzon, George Nathaniel, *Frontiers*, 8008/cc/41, 1907, pp. 5–6.

OIOC, Lockhart, William, *Letter to Secretary of State of the Government of India*, 1898.

OIOC L/PS/10/42 *Political and Secret Department*, pp. 47–55.

OIOC, Cunningham, George, *Private Correspondence*, 1947.

OIOC, European Manuscripts, Mss Eur D670/6.

OIOC, European Manuscripts, Mss Eur D714/70.

Reports and Journals

Aziz, Khalid, *Frontier Crimes Regulation and Administration of the Tribal Areas, Government of India Regulation No. III, 1901*.

Bangash, Mumtaz A., *FATA: Towards a New Beginning*, paper in *Tribal Areas of Pakistan*, Islamabad Policy Research Institute, Islamabad, 2005.

Farrell, Thomas D., 'The Founding of the North-West Frontier Militias', *Journal of the Royal Central Asian Society*, June 1972.

General Staff Army Headquarters, *A Dictionary of the Pathan Tribes of the North-West Frontier of India*, Superintendent Government Printing, Calcutta, 1910.

Howell, Evelyn, *A Monograph on Government's Relations with the Mahsud Tribe*, Government of India Press, Simla, 1931.

Hussain, Ijaz, 'Is the Durand Agreement Dead?' paper in *Tribal Areas of Pakistan: Challenges and Responses*, Islamabad Policy Research Institute, Islamabad, 2005.

Kundi, Mansoor Akbar, *Federally Administered Tribal Areas of Pakistan*, Asia Printers, Islamabad Policy Research Institute, Islamabad, 2005.

Omissi, David, 'The RAF in Iraq and India in the 1920s', *The Journal of the T.E. Lawrence Society*, vol. XIII, No. 2.

Stein, Aurel, 'Notes on Tirah', *Journal of the Royal Asiatic Society*, London, July 1925.

Secondary Sources

Allen, Charles, *Soldier Sahibs*, Abacus, London, 2001.

——, *God's Terrorists*, Little Brown, London, 2006.

185

Baha, Lal, *N.W.F.P. Administration under British Rule*, National Commission on Historical and Cultural Research, Islamabad, 1978.

Banerjee, Mukulika, *The Pathan Unarmed*, Oxford University Press, Karachi, 2000.

Barthorp, Michael, *The North-West Frontier*, Blanford Press, Dorset, 1982.

——, *The Frontier Ablaze*, Windrow & Greene, London, 1996.

——, *Afghan Wars*, Cassell & Co., London, 1982.

Barton, William, *India's North-West Frontier*, John Murray, London, 1939.

Beaumont, Roger, *Sword of the Raj*, Bobbs-Merrill Co., Inc., Indianapolis, 1977.

Caroe, Olaf, *The Pathans*, Macmillan & Co., London, 1958.

Chevenix Trench, Charles, *The Frontier Scouts*, Jonathan Cape, London, 1985.

Churchill, Winston, *The Story of the Malakand Field Force*, Leo Cooper, London, 2002 (original by Longmans, 1898).

——, *My Early Life*, Eland Publishing, London, 2000 (first published in 1930).

Davies, Collin C., *The Problem of the North-West Frontier*, Curzon Press, London, 1932.

Durand, Algernon, *The Making of a Frontier*, Oxford University Press, Karachi, 2004 (first published by Thomas Nelson & Sons).

Edwardes, Michael, *The Last Years of British India*, Nel Mentor, London, 1967.

——, *The Necessary Hell*, Cassell & Co., London, 1958.

Elliott, James G., *The Frontier 1839–1947*, Cassell, London, 1968.

Elphinstone, Monstuart, *An Account of the Kingdom of Caubal*, Indus Publications, Karachi (originally published in 1808).

Fraser-Tytler, Kerr, *Afghanistan*, Oxford University Press, London, 1950.

Hensman, Howard, *The Afghan War of 1879–80*, Sang-e-Meel Publications, Lahore, 1999.

Hodson, R.V.E., *The Story and Gallantry of the North-West Frontier*, Clio Publishing, Southampton, 2002.

Holdich, Thomas, *The Indian Borderland*, Methuen & Co., London, 1901.

Hosseine, Khaled, *The Kite Runner*, Bloomsbury, London, 2003.

Jalalzai, Musa Khan, *The Foreign Policy of Afghanistan*, Sang-e-Meel, Lahore, 2003.

James, Lawrence, *Raj: The Making of British India*, Little, Brown & Co., London, 1997.

Keppel, Arnold, *Gun Running and the Indian North-West Frontier*, Sang-e-Meel Publications, Lahore, 2004.

King, Peter, *The Viceroy's Fall*, Sidgwick & Jackson, London, 1986.

Leeson, Frank, *Frontier Legion*, The Leeson Archive (privately printed), 2003.

Macmunn, George, *Afghanistan from Darius to Amanullah*, Sang-e-Meel Publications, Lahore, 2002.

Mason, Philip, *A Matter of Honour*, Jonathan Cape, London, 1988.

Masters, John, *Bugles and a Tiger*, Michael Joseph, London, 1956.

Miller, Charles, *Khyber*, Macdonald & Jane's, London, 1977.

Nevill, H.L., *Campaigns on the North-West Frontier*, Sang-e-Meel Publications, Lahore, 2003 (original edition 1910).

O'Ballance, Edgar, *Afghan Wars*, Oxford University Press, Oxford, 2003.

Oliver, Edward, *Across the Border*, Chapman and Hall, London, 1890.

Paget, W.H. and Mason, A.H., *Record of Expeditions against the North-West Frontier Tribes*, Whiting & Co., London, 1884.

Pennell, Thomas, *Among the Wild Tribes of the Afghan Frontier*, Seeley & Co., London, 1909.

Rahman, Abdur, *The Life of Abdur Rahman*, John Murray, London, 1900.

Rashid, Ahmed, *Taliban*, I.B. Tauris, London, 2002.

Roberts, Frederick, *Forty-one Years in India*, Macmillan & Co., London, 1914.

Robson, Brian, *Crisis on the Frontier*, Spellmount, Kent, 2004.

Salim, Ahmad, *Loya Jirga*, Sang-e-Meel Publications, Lahore, 2006.

Sayeed, Khalid B., *The Political System of Pakistan*, Houghton, Mifflin, New York, 1967.

Schofield, Victoria, *Old Road, New Highways*, Oxford University Press, Karachi, 1997.

Shah, Sayed, Wiqar Ali, *Ethnicity, Islam and Nationalism*, Oxford University Press, Karachi, 1999.

Skeen, General Sir Andrew, *Passing it On*, Gale & Polden Ltd., London, 1932.

Spain, James W., *The Pathan Borderland*, Indus Publications, Karachi, 1963.

Starr, Lillian, *Tales of Tirah and Lesser Tibet*, Hodder and Stoughton, London, 1924.

Stewart, Jules, *The Savage Border*, Sutton Publishing Ltd., Stroud, 2007.

Tanner, Stephen, *Afghanistan: A Military History from Alexander the Great to the Fall of the Taliban*, Oxford University Press, Karachi, 2002.

Thapar, Romila, *Early India*, Penguin, London, 2002.

Thorburn, S.S., *Bannu, or Our Afghan Frontier*, Sang-e-Meel Publications, Lahore, 1999.

Toynbee, Arnold, *Between Oxus and Jumna*, Oxford University Press, London, 1961.

Villiers-Stuart, J.P., *Letters of a Once Punjab Frontier Force Officer*, Sifton, London, 1925.

Warburton, Robert, *Eighteen Years in the Khyber*, John Murray, London, 1900.

Woodruff, Philip, *The Men Who Ruled India*, Jonathan Cape, London, 1953.

Younghusband, George, *The Story of the Guides*, Macmillan and Co., London, 1918.

Index